THE
E.L.L.E.R.

(Experiencing Long-Lasting and Enjoyable Relationships)

MODEL

OREN L. HARRIS

PAGE PUBLISHING, INC.
New York, NY

First originally published by Page Publishing, Inc. 2018

ISBN 978-1-64214-933-3 (Paperback)
ISBN 978-1-64214-934-0 (Digital)

Printed in the United States of America

To my children and family
To my spiritual family
To my human family
May the seeds in this book make the ELLER flourish in your life.

CONTENTS

Acknowledgments

I wish to express gratitude to my mother whose experience with finding love and understanding of "love flow" inspired the writing of this book.

I want to thank my wife, Joan Harris, for her incredible insights and support throughout this project.

I'm grateful to Milton Dyer, Lana Carter, Linda Felcone, Lisa Arbitell, Gena Clark, Lyn Wilson, Arlene Heckman, and many others who gave their time leading up to the writing of this book.

My thanks to Linda Hogan for editing my book.

My profound and heartfelt gratitude to my professor Jerry Luftman and to Lou Fisher and Louise Marley, my writing teachers with Longridge Writers Institute. Without these three people, I would have never been able to begin thinking about writing this book.

I'm particularly grateful to my many counselees that I have had the privilege of working with over the years. I'm also grateful for the diversity of people that I met while working for limousine companies who shared their personal experiences and feedback with me. The names and details about real-life counseling cases and car conversations included in the book have been changed to maintain confidentiality.

Thanks to my many friends who encouraged and believed in me during the writing of this book.

Finally, I would like to thank God for the inspiration and beauty that gave life to the ELLER model and this book.

To My daughter Denise Harris for designing the cover of ELLER.

INTRODUCTION

If you stop long enough and think about it, there are many kinds of love. And there are many different words and ways to express love. Most people long to express love in a romantic relationship with a compatible partner. For the most part, healthy, loving, and lasting relationships don't come naturally. They don't always happen overnight despite what you see in romantic movies or read in novels.

This book is a primer designed to make you stop, reflect on, and explore the mystery of "heart love" and how love makes you behave. Whether you're floundering or flourishing in your relationships—romantic, parental, workplace, friendships, and everything else in between, this book is written with you in mind. Now, as you can imagine, there's no shortage of books written on relationship management. So why read my book? Good question. Keep reading, and I hope it won't take you long for you to find out why. I believe this book offers a simple approach and alternative perspective on building, maintaining, and enjoying not just a satisfying partnership but also a loving and long-lasting and enjoyable relationship. What's the difference? Keep reading.

The way we communicate and connect with one another is often a challenge and can present a huge stumbling block in most relationships. What would happen if a man couldn't open up to his wife and honestly share his heart? What if a woman repeatedly nagged her husband until he finally shut down? The purpose of this little book is to help you and your loved one understand how to find love perfectly, get love flowing and keep it going in your life. Whether you're married, entering into a committed relationship, or going on your first date, let me show you how to find love perfectly and have long-lasting and enjoyable relationships.

According to the US Census Bureau, there are 100 million Americans searching for that special someone to spend their lives with. Finding love is an important part of everyone's story. Once there is a man who is lonely and longing for love. In that same town, there is a woman who lives alone and looking for love. They happen to meet one day and decide to make a date to see each other again. And they've been seeing each other ever since. For many people, traditional dating means there will be a "happily ever after" ending to their story.

But not everyone finds love through an unexpected meeting or on a blind date. For that reason, people are turning to high-tech options to make a love connection. If you've experimented with online dating, you're not alone. At last count, about forty million people are logging onto Match, a popular dating website. Online dating websites are experiencing competition from dating apps, especially among young adults. They're downloading popular dating apps like Tinder and Bumble in search of true love. Why? They consider dating apps expedient and less intimidating than asking a total stranger out on a date or getting set up on a blind date.

With so many people looking for love, it's no wonder the search is complex and confusing. Enter the ELLER model. Ever wonder what makes or breaks a romantic relationship? I have. That's what made me develop a relationship management model that makes it possible for you and your child, spouse, friend, or partner to overcome your differences and find a way to grow closer and forge lasting connections.

Not familiar with the ELLER model? It stands for Experiencing Long-Lasting and Enjoyable Relationships. This relationship model is based on countless counseling sessions and interviews that have been percolating in my head for the past twenty years in my practice as a counselor. The birth of the ELLER model and the motivation for writing this book became my passion after seeing my mother deal with extramarital affairs. Only after failing in my own marriage did I begin to understand that there is a common thread running in both of our experiences. In different ways, my mother and I found ourselves struggling to let love flow. It's the ability to give and receive love. Just like the wave after wave flows from the ocean to the shore, that's the same way that our love flow should be—effortlessly, faithfully, and consistently.

The concept behind the ELLER model started in 1996 when divorce, affairs, and brokenheartedness had become the norm and a growing epidemic in our society. Back then, the idea of enjoying passionate, healthy, and lifelong relationships seemed like a myth; for many today, it still does. This is also around the same time emotional intelligence—which relies on connecting the mind, emotion, brain, and body in order to understand human behavior—began to rise in popularity. Since then, similar thinking and models have advanced in the field of emotional intelligence that focuses on identifying your emotions and the emotions of others around you to better understand what and why you feel the way you do. Building on this methodology, I believe the ELLER model offers a more reliable and simpler approach to resolving relationships problems and pitfalls.

The ELLER model offers the opportunity for you to find love perfectly, repair relationship problems and restore wounded hearts. Take Maggie, a thirty-year-old woman, who has been struggling with the same relationship problem. No longer capable of living with her boyfriend, Maggie decides to leave and move into her mother's house. Despite Maggie and her boyfriend having a contentious relationship, she feels lonely without him. Eventually, Maggie relents and moves back with her boyfriend. When asked why she made her decision, she replies, "I was lonely." When asked if she has resolved the problems in their relationship and sex life, Maggie gets quiet, starts crying, and then replies, "I was … lonely."

Finding love again is possible for Maggie and so many others who have been unsuccessful in addressing their relationship issues on their own. Maggie would have been benefitted by putting the five stages of the ELLER model into practice to

- identify and analyze your process for finding love;
- detect fractures or breaks in your relationship in order to better understand yourself and the love you wish to find;

- put the ELLER principles into practice and let love flow from your heart to your partner;
- bring healing from emotional damage; and
- restore and release into freedom.

Damaged Goods

Maybe you've never thought of it this way, but every human being is made up of a nine part system—the mind, emotions, will, spirit, heart (not our physical heart that pumps blood to our body but the emotional one that keeps love flowing perfectly), mouth, brain, body and skin. When you identify and understand how all these parts are interrelated, the greater opportunity you have of finding love and becoming empowered to receive and give love. And in the physical body, there are three parts that contribute to empowerment—the skin, brain, and mouth (See "The Nine-Part Human Theory" chapter).

Messy breakup. Job loss. Unexpected diagnosis. Childhood trauma. Deep disappointment. These can leave a person feeling unloved, wounded, unworthy, or unwanted. Perhaps sometime in your life you've experienced one or all of these feelings. The pain you feel after a broken relationship, loss, or traumatic experience can cause you to doubt if anyone else will ever love you. Does your pain make you feel like damaged goods? The dictionary defines damaged goods this way: "A person who is impaired, corrupted, or defiled."

Without empowerment, you may continue to think of yourself as damaged goods. Is the damage irreparable? Growing up, children observe their parents or guardian giving love, experiencing love, and responding to the quantity and quality of love they received from us.

What's Love Anyway?

A woman exclaimed, "What's love anyway?" Women who say that could be disappointed in finding love, heartbroken over a lover, can't find love perfectly, emotionally damaged, frustrated about a relationship, don't love themselves … and more. I find that 90% of women knows and understand what love is, while 10% of women are damaged by 90% of men and are not sure what Love is anymore. 90% of men are not sure what Love is, while 10% of them knows what Love is. Eg. The term 90% man or woman is representative of 90% of men or women. Understanding and defining love is as daunting as understanding and defining life. You can't find something you don't understand. God is love, which makes the spirit the most important part of us. Based on the model, there are three parts of love—the empowering love, the hard part of love, and the easy part of love, the easy part of is sex. The empowering part of love is the activated, spirited heart, which leads to the hard kind of love (which is heart-to-heart communication—sharing and listening to their hearts.) All these parts of love work together in relationships.

What's love anyway? "What's love got to do with it?" here is an example, "LOML" brings a 90 percent woman and a 10 percent man together. Both share openly, so there are no surprises. And they're both good listeners and empowered and activated spirit in their hearts. If an emergency occurs, they are there for each other. That demonstrates an extreme sense of loyalty, consistency, and dependability without codependency.

When people cut themselves, they do what they know they shouldn't do—staying with a man who physically abuses his spouse and refusing to get help and drinking excessive alcohol continuously but not admitting they need help. Do they love themselves? Refusing to love yourself makes it impossible to put the ELLER model to work in your relationships. Coming to grips with your identity takes you one step closer to breaking free from emotional damage from childhood or a traumatic event that recently happened. As a result of past experiences, you may think of yourself as damaged goods. That damage varies from person to person. The nine-part human theory is critical to correcting any damage and learning what's love anyway.

The 90/10 matrix is mandatory to banish loneliness and remove the "damaged goods" label from you. This matrix (explained in greater detail in "The 90/10 Matrix" chapter) helps couples determine whether the love in their relationship needs to be rekindled.

Relationships work best when there is a healthy balance, a give and take. Sonny and Peggy (a 90 percent man and 90 percent woman) are a great example. Peggy loves to take her time in everything she does including their relationship. Sonny, on the other hand, moves fast in everything he does, whether it's talking or lovemaking. Peggy enjoys emotional and physical foreplay leading up to lovemaking, but her partner doesn't. She confesses that she would gain greater pleasure from intercourse and climaxing if more time was spent on foreplay. Heart-to-heart communication involving a 90 percent woman and 10 percent man is all about taking things slow and enjoying the process. Ninety percent men insist on moving at warp speed with or without their partner, because intimacy scares them. To reveal what's in their hearts and on their minds, they have to be vulnerable.

A couple's differences influence them on finding love and how love flows in their relationships. Doris is a twenty-five-year-old who is a 90 percent woman. Married to a 90 percent man, she finds emotional and physical foreplay more pleasurable than he does. Why is this? She seems scared, feels unsafe with her husband who moves too fast, and struggles with sharing her heart with him.

It isn't unusual for a 90 percent man to avoid talking about his feelings (based on the heart-and-mouth connection outlined in "The Nine-Part Human Theory" chapter). He is full of pride and refuses to discuss his hurts, pain, past, struggles, fears, anxiety, and worries.

Married to a 90 percent woman, there is always the potential for the couple to clash in their relationship. As their relationship continues, the 90 percent woman begins to adopt behavior traits that are the exact opposite of her partner. She loves to share her heart—and talk about her feelings, pain, hurt, struggles, and deeply desires her man to do the same. Most marriages are between 90 percent men and 90 percent women; that's the reason why there is so many broken hearts, divorce, separation, and affairs, and love is no longer flowing like it used to.

The 10 percent woman once was a 90 percent woman. After marrying a 90 percent man, she was worn down by him and soon became a 10 percent woman. (See the "Relationship Degradation Curve" chapter and discussion of the degradation of most relationship curves.) Early in the relationship, she openly shared her heart, but emotional damage took its toll on her heart and emotions. The first phase of damage happened when she moved in together with her 90 percent man. Sharing residence is often one of the first places where conflicts emerge and clashes in the decision-making process occur.

With nowhere to go with hurt feelings, she reluctantly buried them deep inside her heart—every woman's hidden databank. Similar conflicts developed as she aged. Conflicts increases as both worked and allowed the emotional hurt to widen the gap between them. The more distance, the more conflicts, the more she morphs into a 10 percent woman. This scenario is exacerbated when factoring the emotional baggage from her upbringing.

Love at first sight is very possible, but how many love-at-first-sight marriages end up in divorce court? Nevertheless, love at first sight is impacted by the brain, emotion, and spirit. Initially, this response to your partner is something that you feel and think about on a deep spiritual level. The ELLER model identifies the traditional three levels of love differently (see "The ELLER Model" chapter).

What's love anyway? It takes more than falling in love and love at first sight to produce ELLER. The same goes for your soulmate. People who find their soulmate can still end up getting divorced.

THE ELLER MODEL

Dream of having the ideal relationship? What's holding your heart back from living out your dream? Fear of failure? A painful past? Just like an X-ray machine, the ELLER model doesn't simply scratch the surface of your relationships; it penetrates deep into the heart. The model is designed for you to find love perfectly, keep love flowing, and strengthen your relationships. The model's goal is to prevent breakups and heartaches from occurring and to safeguard marriages from extramarital affairs and divorce. Five key here are the components that drive the ELLER model:

- The nine-part human theory
- 90/10 matrix
- 80/20 model
- Relationship degradation curve
- types of model-based love

Using the ELLER model not only gives you the opportunity to peer into another person's heart but reveals how the nine functions of your being flow/operate together. It gives a "window" needed to look and get to know about someone in order to find love perfectly and keep love flowing.

One of the most frequently asked questions about the ELLER model is, *Are some relationships/marriages just never meant to be?* Simply put, never give up on repairing a relationship or fixing a marriage as long as there is one willing to make the commitment work.

The ELLER model isn't limited to love flow with couples. It can also strengthen relationships with friends, parents and children, and coworkers. Johanna, a forty-five-year-old single parent/mom, put the model to work with her daughter. She now has the capability of penetrating her seventeen-year-old daughter's heart and actively listening to what she has to say. But often, what is most revealing remains unspoken; that is what her teenager is really thinking and feeling. Like peeling back layers of an onion, the model encourages asking open-ended, noninvasively with persistence and love. For example, by weaving open-ended and nonthreatening questions into conversations, parents, spouses, and friends can drill down until they discover the root of the problem. "What's wrong?" or "What was your day like?" or "Want to talk about it later?" or "What happened when you did this before?" "How might that change the way you do things?" These are all questions that allow you to learn more than you expected. Your children might share about issues you never knew existed, uncensored stories, and unanticipated answers. By asking short and deliberate questions, Johanna's daughter no longer feels she has to limit her response. By understanding the heart-heart connection, then you realize that threatening, critical, and combative questions will only shut down the lines of communication between your teenager, spouse, or loved one. Johanna also learned to avoid invasive behavior, such as the blame game, complaints or put downs.

The more open, nonthreatening questions, the more your loved one's heart will melt and they will realize you care about their well-being. They will also accept that your love for them is genuine, from the heart.

Vulnerability and the ELLER Model

At the heart of the ELLER model, there is the powerful concept called vulnerability. It's the freedom to be yourself. Being vulnerable is what's missing in most relationships. Without vulnerability, there is no trust, intimacy, or love. The ELLER model gives you and your partner the courage to fight against fears that prevent the two of you from being real and raw. The following are relationship issues addressed by the model:

- *Facing your fears.* Some people are willing to face fear head-on. They make the choice to take a risk, let down their guard, and trust their partners. Conversely, others are paralyzed by fear. Overcoming fear can seem as daunting and dangerous as climbing atop Mount Everest. So they think it's better to play it safe. Working through the model will show them how you tackle their massive mountain of fears, the unknown, failure, disappointment, and more.
- *Stop hiding your heart.* Vulnerability is quite often viewed as a sign of weakness, especially by men, but it's really not. Actually, it takes strength to admit you're not perfect and that you have flaws. Instead of hiding your heart, the model will help you keep love flowing by sharing what's in your heart without reservation.
- *Risking rejection.* Don't shy away from vulnerability because of what someone might think or say if they really knew

you. If you can't be vulnerable, then you can't truly grow and be your best self. Without exposing your thoughts, beliefs, and feelings, not only will your relationship lack love or trust but also intimacy. Creating long-lasting and enjoyable relationships is why the model was created.

Like superglue, vulnerability is what bonds couples together, reinforcing closeness, connection, and commitment between you and your partner or loved one.

Navigating the ups and downs of any relationship can be frustrating. That's especially true when it comes to romantic love. Relationship problems are what prompted Barbara to share her feelings. What started off as a guarded conversation between two strangers soon turns into an honest dialogue about the relationship differences she is having with her forty-two-year-old boyfriend. When talking about what keeps couples from embracing vulnerability, I noticed how frequently Barbara's words (based on honest and candid thoughts) lined up perfectly with her heart (the real emotions and past hurts).

Barbara begins by asking, "So, the ELLER model can help me and my boyfriend, right?"

"Do you love him?" I ask.

"Yes, he's the one," she replies. "I know it, but I have started to hold back. I'm not as vulnerable with him as I was when we first met, and it has reduced our desire for sex. What do I do? How can the ELLER model help so we can know we have found love perfectly?"

I explained that love has three parts, which are all interrelated. "First, there's the empowering part (finding love perfectly) that equips you to embrace the hard part (being vulnerable), and then facilitates the easy part (love flow that leads to good sex). You and your boyfriend are having problems with the easy part, sex. Tell me about him."

"He is going to therapy," she adds, "but he doesn't want to share what is happening with me."

"So he is not being vulnerable, right?"

"Yes!" Barbara answers. After hearing about the model, she continues, "I have some hope now that I know that it's possible to know when I have found love perfectly. I see now what you mean when you say I could have empowerment and a healthy relationship. But if I step in and take control of our relationship, I run the risk of influencing things instead of sharing the responsibility with him. And as a result, he winds up contributing less and less to our relationship. He was always a 90 percent man, but now he's disengaged and is only investing less and less of himself."

I explain, "His problem could stem from environmental, physiological, psychological, or theological, or a combination of each."

We agreed to continue our discussion later that day. After numerous text messages back and forth, Barbara is feeling hopeful again about finding love perfectly and restoring their relationship. A door of hope opens when she decided to take risks and stop allowing fear to control her. Our dialogue eventually reveals she has been wrestling with a specific problem and needs help dealing with it.

"He loves his erection and does not climax sometimes even though I climax. He blames me that we are out of sync," admits Barbara. "He says sex is important to him, and he does not want to get married to me and wind up divorcing me over it. The second problem is that sometimes I can't get him to share his heart. Otherwise, he is a perfect guy."

"He is having a problem with the hardest part of love, being vulnerable," I say. "Vulnerability is what facilitates the easy part of love, good sex and love flow. Both of you climaxing and enjoying foreplay, intercourse, and cuddling is what the ELLER model is designed to facilitate."

Barbara pauses and adds, "He doesn't like foreplay. He just wants to go straight to intercourse."

"Does that bother you?"

"Yes," she says.

"Three strikes so far ..."

"I know, I know. How do I fix this?" Barbara says. "He is the one for me. I know it."

"It's going to take a power greater than you or your boyfriend to fix this. In the nine-part human system, there is a critical component called the spirit that empowers people. It is the spirit that empowers people. It's the spirit that changes, activates, and transforms every part of who we are; our heart, mind, emotion, body, will, brain, mouth, and skin. Connecting with the spirit can help your boyfriend make the shift from stonewalling to sharing his heart and becoming more vulnerable and willingness to please you with foreplay."

What makes Barbara share her struggles with a perfect stranger? Maybe she simply has grown tired of walking on eggshells around her partner, protecting herself so he wouldn't fully know her and her true feelings. She finally makes a brave move that leads her to let go of being in control and fear of the unknown. Using the ELLER model, Barbara now better understands why she no longer can simply remain silent, and keep her emotions and self-defeating thoughts locked up. In the short time that we talked, Barbara has gone through a major transformation. She learns the importance of standing up for herself and freely give and fully receive love from her partner. The ELLER model has guided Barbara step-by-step through acting on what she wanted in their relationship instead of closing her heart and distancing herself again from her boyfriend. If the model could do all this in a day for Barbara, what could it do in a week, a month, or even a year for you and your spouse/partner?

The Nine-Part Human System

There are nine parts of our being that (aren't body parts) that transcend all cultures, genders, ethnic background, and races. They're essential to finding love perfectly, keep love flowing, and experience empowerment. The mind, spirit, will, emotions, heart, body, skin, mouth, brain. All these parts are connected. Five are intangible—our heart, mind, spirit, emotions, and will. The skin is the largest body part. The heart is controller over all the parts. The spirit is like a muscle that has to be exercised to ensure its effectiveness.

Martha best illustrates the significance of the mouth-and-heart connection. She is a 90 percent woman, and her mate is a 90 percent man. She opened up her heart and talked to a 10 percent man outside her marriage about her relationship struggles and sex life. The 10 percent man knew how to get Martha to open up her heart and even more. When Martha is asked if she talks to her husband so openly, she laughs and says, "Hell no!" The 10 percent man doesn't know, but this behavior would cause Martha's Relationship curve (RDC Relationship degradation curve) to decline. She's feeling emotionally good about what happened, so her heart sends messages to the brain and hormones are released in her bloodstream and infiltrates her skin making her vulnerable and susceptible to making bad decisions that affects her marriage. The mouth starts the whole system in motion.

The Spirit

Spirit is a concept that declares power over the mind. The ELLER model is based on empowerment and influence. The spirit is conceptual (and embraces everyone's thinking). If anything good happens to a person, and the mind cannot figure out how it happens, then it is the spirit that is in charge of that transaction. The spirit is like the sun; it shines on everyone or at least wills to shine on everyone, so the sun is like a big spirit that has a will, a big will. An individual can, of their own will, choose to stay out of the sun with their own will but eventually to their detriment. So the big spirit—the sun—as it were, overrides the will of the little spirit. Ultimately the big spirit is the source of power. The spirit in the ELLER model is resident in the heart and acts just like a muscle. It needs to be activated in order to work out. The spirit is the only part of the system that can help the heart which makes decision to Find Love. Many find love that end up in divorce, heart brokenness and affairs. The activated spirit in the heart is what produces empowerment and influence in the ELLER model.

The Heart

The heart, not the physical heart, controls the nine-part system of love. Some call it the emotional heart. The heart is where all the hurt, pain, disappointments, and emotional damage is stored. The heart is connected to the mouth, and if the heart is closed, then that is why it is difficult for some people to talk (with the mouth) about what's in their heart.

The heart finds love for us. Molly was cheery and chatty for twenty minutes until I share the ELLER model. As a counselor, using the ELLER model, I could tell what's in Molly's heart by simply listening to what comes out of her mouth and observing her body language (See Appendix for nonfictional story "Nightmare in a Crater" based on actual counseling sessions and "Die or I Will Kill You.") Molly said, "Now I am nervous!" For the next twenty minutes, she has no response to the ELLER model—no mention of a husband or boyfriend. She abruptly closes her heart and that's why she stops speaking. Some people would also change the subject. When the heart is pleased, good mood follows. When the heart is hurt, bad mood follows. "A happy wife is a happy life," they say when a wife's heart is not clogged up with pain and unresolved conflicts she is happy and the man is too. When a woman's heart is filled with pain and unresolved conflicts, it leads to shut down and hardening of her heart and no love flow.

The Skin

The skin focuses on the touch, skin-on-skin, cuddling, fondling, holding, and caressing. Touching starts in the womb and continues as we age into adulthood. Skin-on-skin touch is most important to relationship development and behavior. The most enjoyably perfect relationship ever is between a mother and child in the womb. Touching the skin is a very important nonverbal communication where messages are sent in a relationship. The skin is a tactile organ. The skin has sensors that are connected to the nervous system, spinal cord, and the brain. When the skin is touched, the brain records, interprets the touch, and sends signals/messages to the mind, emotion, heart, will, and mouth; all nine part system of the human theory gets involved. The skin is a tactile organ that's sensuous. In a Caribbean paradise where there are open windows, a thirty-year-old wife can be heard saying, "Shelly! Shelly! Shelly! Oh, Shelly! On and on for ten minutes as the skin-on-skin operation of sex the easy part of love was in process. The precursor to the skin-on-skin was kissing in the mouth—more skin on skin, a very important part of foreplay and love flow. Hugging, cuddling, and holding hands are skin movement. The ecstasy by both husband and wife in oral sex is another skin on skin that arouses and moves all nine part system of the being into action. It is recommended that couples arriving home at the end of the day hug for one minute even without kissing. It is amazing what could result later in the bedroom if that skin-on-skin touching were followed by more couples.

When a woman says, "Don't touch me!" What is going on besides she doesn't want to be physically touched? A woman sleeping on the edge of the bed or sleeping on the couch or in another room sends the same message. Touch is the language of the skin. The skin is repulsed because the eight other parts of the nine-part system are affected. There is what she is thinking (the mind) about how she was probably abused by a husband, say a 90 percent husband. She is unraveling, emotionally exploding. Her heart has been hurt, damaged, and she is not telling you what the damage is by those words; she is storing the damage information in her heart, no mouth movement to talk about it. She has exercised her will to not share what's bothering her. She is not in a spirit good state. Her spirit could not be activated. Her brain has stopped releasing hormones of pleasure and desire. Her body doesn't want to be touched. The desire, readiness for sex, the easy part of love, is out the window. A man having empowerment and understanding of the nine-part theory, can still produce ELLER in this scenario.

The Mouth

The mouth is the part through which we share, speak, and talk about what's in our heart. The mouth is highlighted because it is the most direct way; of sharing what is in the heart. What is stored in the heart is pain, disappointments, emotional damage, weaknesses, struggles, hurts, and feelings acquired from our environmental existence developed from childhood. When a woman says to her husband you don't talk, she is referring to using the mouth to express what's lodged in her heart.

The Will

The will is included as part of the nine-part human system because it's the place where decisions are made. The will makes the decisions that the mind processes and the emotions feels. The will is stripped out apart from the mind because it gives us a deeper understanding of BCR theory—why people behave the way they do. All this contributes to the development of the ELLER model.

The Emotion

Emotion is the feeling part of the system. You hear, "I don't feel like it." "I'm not feeling good." "That doesn't make me feel good." "I feel turned on. I feel happy." "I feel great." The emotion is connected to the mind, heart, and spirit, which causes emotion to be released. In Behavior Communications Relationship (BCR) theory, our emotions—both the good and the bad—are the most volatile part of the system.

The Mind

The mind is the logical agent of our behavior system. The complexity and beauty of the mind has sent men to the moon and discovered life-saving inventions, but there are still many things the mind can't figure out and fix. Poverty is one example. So the mind in the ELLER model is labeled limited.

The Body

The body is one of the most obvious part of system. Body language in communication theory highlights the importance of the body, even though communication goes way beyond body language. The body and its importance are seen in intimate relationships and sex (the easy part of love). When the heart and mind and spirit are not involved in the easy part of love, then the body doesn't cooperate.

The Brain

The brain connection and function are seen when the heart is stimulated; then true listening and sharing between a husband and wife as in heart-to-heart communication begins. The brain then receives messages from the heart (as in when a woman gets "turned on"), and sends and releases hormones to the physical heart and bloodstream. Therein lies one of the most important functions of the system and the BCR theory.

THE 90/10 MATRIX

Finding your LOML (Love of my life) is Finding Love Perfectly.

The 90/10 matrix categorizes all women and men across all races, cultures, gender, and ethnic origin to deepen the understanding of the behavior-communication-relationship problems. The percent type depicts the percentage of... Eg. 90 percent man means 90 percent of men. The behavior of a 90 percent man is similar to the actions of a 10 percent woman, while a 90 percent woman resembles the actions of a 10 percent man. A 90 percent woman knows how to open up her heart and candidly share feelings, weaknesses, and struggles. She listens intently with an open heart and engages in conversation with eye contact and without any distractions or interruptions and affirms with one word like yep, ok. which shows that she is listening. A 10 percent man has the same ability, but a 90 percent man doesn't. Ten percent of women once had this ability until they were negatively affected by 90 percent men.

Believe it or not, 100 percent of women are looking for 10 percent men who are hard to find, so they compromise and go with a 90% man due to loneliness, biological clock and social pressures. This move later come back to bite them. 90 percent men and 90 percent women makes up the majority of marriages. Most divorces, affairs, and heartbreaks are found when 90 percent men get together with 90 percent women. Marriages that last forty, fifty, or sixty years occur among 90 percent women and 10 percent men who rely on the ELLER model. A 10 percent woman and a 90 percent man can have relationships but are only together for convenience with little or no intimacy, living like roommates and relating as friends; not even good friends. Many 90 percent women end up compromising and settling for a 90 percent man. This move creates a difficulty for these 90 percent women. A key part of the nine-part human theory is connection between the heart (where all the data of our lives is stored) and the mouth. Of particular note are the bad things that have happened to the person's life from their environment. Ninety percent of men have problems talking about what's in their heart. Ten percent of women's hearts have been damaged by 90 percent men that they too have problems recovering from their painful past and wounded hearts. For them, the 90 percent men could have been their dad, guardian, boyfriends, or ex-husband(s). Heart-to-heart communications is vital to ELLER. Keep in mind that many relationships are long-lasting but not enjoyable or not as enjoyable as when the person found love or think they found love. In many cases, people do not find love perfectly as you can with ELLER. Many relationships too are enjoyable, but couples have no confidence that their relationship will be long-lasting because they don't have a "model" to give them that assurance. There are business and scientific models that does great things and accomplish great feats. Look around and there are not too many relationship models, if any. If so, check to see if love and empowerment is there to understand behavior, foster communications, and assure long-lasting and enjoyable relationships. A 90 percent man can be influenced to change to a 10 percent man by an empowered 90 percent woman, and a 10 percent woman can be influenced to change to a 90 percent woman by the empowerment of a 10 percent man.

Relationship Degradation Curve

Anger, disagreements, resentment, quarreling—everything is fine one moment, then both of you are at odds and fighting the next. Conflict happens. It is natural and a normal part of life. Whether you are best friends, parents, new to dating, engaged, newlyweds, or married for decades, it's impossible to have a long-term relationship without conflicts. Just because two people argue, that doesn't mean they don't care about or love each other. The potential for conflict exists whenever people have different needs, values, or interests.

Conflict can either create deeper understanding, closeness, and respect, or it can be destructive and put a wedge between people that can lead to bitterness, hostility, breakups, or divorce. Finding ways of resolving a conflict so that it satisfies your needs, as well as your partner's, is challenging but you should strive toward that goal. The ELLER model gives you the tools and nonthreatening language to identify the root problem and resolve the conflict.

There is no simple straight line to follow that will take you to your destination—achieving a loving, long-lasting, and healthy relationship with your spouse/partner. Sooner or later, every couples make a wrong turn, hits a bump in the road, or encounters an unexpected detour. That's why the relationship degradation curve (RDC) is essential to our model. The RDC is a relationship curve and everyone wants their curve to be linear. The curve depicts the increasing pain that unresolved conflicts can produce and the different conflict points over a relationship life.

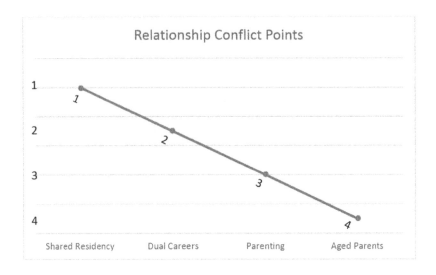

When one or all four relationship conflict points are in unre-solved mode, you may feel your relationship isn't progressing like it once did. Remember, growth isn't always linear. For every mountain peak, there is a deeper valley. For every leap forward, there is a stumble backward. Sometimes, one step. Maybe, even two or three. Missteps, mistakes, and misunderstandings—they all have an effect on you whether or not the "curve" of your relationship is on the incline or decline. If couples feel embattled in the same unresolved conflicts year after year after year, they will soon find the weight of the heart-break, disappointment, take a toll on their relationship, degrading the progress they once made and derailing them from experiencing a long lasting and enjoyable relationship with love flowing. Now let's take a closer look at the RDC and why and how the four relationship conflict points impact any relationship curve.

1. *Shared residence.* The idea of sharing your home with some-one you love can be scary. Men and women often expect different things when they live together. At the end of the day, you both share a common goal of wanting to live in a space that makes you feel safe, secure, and comfortable.

2. *Dual careers.* Marriage and careers are two of the most important parts of our lives, and making both work in parallel is a top priority. Nearly 50 percent of all American marriages are dual-career couples according to *The Harvard Business Review*. Without a doubt, failure to communicate and differing opinions degrade the RDC. Couples need to make sure they're on the same page. That was the issue that Donovan and Beverly faced. Take Donavan and Beverly for example. They met and found love. Six months later, they decided to move in together. Neither realized how sharing the same residence could change and challenge their relationship. Beverly was excited about fixing up the house, something close to a woman's heart. It didn't take long for her to discover what was in her heart was vastly different than what Donovan had in mind. On the surface, it sounded like Beverly was not just talking about choosing decorations and furniture; what she really was expecting from living together was experiencing love and excitement with her husband. She wanted Donavan to have feelings, thoughts, and plans, but he just wasn't into talking, especially not things that didn't matter to him—like paint colors, carpet samples, or sheet thread counts. So he decided to simply fake listen to his wife. Beverly realized his heart was not in it. Even though he financially supported decorating the house and even went shopping at the mall with her, but the intimacy wasn't there. Donovan's refusal to open up and discuss what was in his heart left Beverly feeling disappointed and lonely. And the situation only got worse as their workload and priorities increased.

3. *Parenting.* Parenting and its conflicts cause even more degradation to the curve. The exhausting demands of parenthood can seem overwhelming. The average parents argue eight times a month about child-rearing. Of course, if you're in a relationship, then you and your partner certainly want to do everything you can to keep your curve going up. Unresolved conflicts over disciplining your child,

lack of sleep or sex, and finances heaped on top of more unresolved conflicts will certainly bring the curve down.

4. *Aged parents.* Caring for an aging parent can be stressful beyond belief. The high cost, doctors' visits, end-of-life care, and balancing caregiving with raising a family can all contribute to brewing up the perfect storm for couples. Keeping your love alive while caring for aging parents can put a strain a marriage or other relationships. Unspoken expectations, hurts, and disappointments can lead to more trouble. When caretakers concentrate completely on senior care, they wind up neglecting their own relationship. When that occurs, their relationship curve will go downhill faster than a runaway train with no conductor. Don't let setbacks derail you. Simply get onboard and get things back on track.

Statistics show that heartbreak, affairs, and divorce happens at various points on the curve. The ELLER model, along with guidance from a well-trained ELLER coach, can help resolve conflicts before they become a crisis. Love flows perfectly whenever your relationship progresses forward and keeps looking up.

The 80/20 Model

The 80/20 model is like a bridge between science/logic and the spirit. (Eighty percent is an arbitrary number to show ratio.) All influence in decision-making and experiencing the ELLER model is from the spirit. Spirit here is conceptual so that it embraces everyone and everyone interested in the ELLER model! Keep in mind we are here on earth for the purpose of the spirit. The spirit is involved in 80 percent of everyone's life. The sun is a great analogy to understand the spirit. It shines on everyone and influences everyone. Some of us, due to our will, avoid exposure to the sun at all costs and with great consequences. Eventually, the person can't avoid the sun any longer and is hit with the heat but also therapeutic benefits of the sunshine. What's left there is a 20% which is the person's responsibility in decision making in order to go out into the sun and experience the benefit of the sun. If you can sit back and do less than your 20 percent, then you'll miss the fulfillment of your purpose. But if you're aggressive and accomplish more than your 20 percent, you will undoubtedly experience anxiety, worry, fear, and feeling overwhelmed. A balanced 80-20 is where ELLER is experienced.

BEHAVIOR-COMMUNICATIONS-RELATIONSHIP CONNECTION

When a woman makes any of these remarks, "Whatever!" "Fine!" "It is what it is!" "Oh well!" What message is she sending? What's going on in her heart? Is love flowing? What's the status of her relationship with her man? These unanswered questions and her 90 percent man's heart may be the reason for the degrading relationship curves, affairs, broken hearts, separations, and divorces in today's society.

FINDING LOVE

What is love anyway? Once you know, then you can find love and find it perfectly and Finding Love is, according to ELLER, the most important pursuit in Life. Divorces, love affairs, broken hearts, separations, and loneliness happen when love is not found and when one thought they found it. (See Appendix for fictional story, "Deafening Cry.") Finding love perfectly is what drives the ELLER model in conjunction with the support of a ELLER mentor or coach.

Caroline is twenty-eight years old and a 90 percent woman wounded in a previous relationship. With the help of the ELLER model and ELLER coaching, she is open to finding love again and perfectly this time. Once she met her 10 percent man, she wants some assurance. Caroline reviews questions about her partner on the ELLER checklist with her ELLER coach:

Was he empowered?

Good listener?

Was his spirit activated in his heart?

Did he share his heart openly and get her to open up hers?

Did he make her feel safe and cherished?

Did he respect her enough to get married first before engaging in sex?

The answer to all these questions was—yes for Meg. She has observed this behavior consistently before opening her heart and emotions to him. She even had gone through premarital therapy with Paul. Thirteen years later and after three children, the ELLER model is still active in their lives.

Love Flow

Once you find love perfectly, then the next thing you need to know is how to keep it flowing. Empowerment is the key factor to accomplish this great feat. Empowerment embodies understanding the stages of the model: the nine-part human theory, 90/10 matrix, what is love anyway, finding love perfectly, degradation curve, and the ongoing role of the spirit-activated heart.

Women say love is flowing during the easy part when emotional foreplay, physical foreplay, sexual intercourse, climax, and cuddling takes place. These factors are addressed in the ELLER model. Emotional foreplay (or emotional intimacy) occurs when a 10 percent or a 90 percent man is influenced by a 90 percent woman whose activated spirit allows her to have a heart-to-heart experience with her man. Nothing is left unsaid. They have each other's full attention with no interruptions or distractions. The couple is engaged and affirm each other through their choice of words, empathetic listening (hearing and understanding the emotions behind what's said), and eye contact. The woman is now ready for physical foreplay because her heart sends a message to her brain. Her brain releases hormones to the blood stream. The release of hormone to the skin heightens the flow. The skin is the largest and most sensitive organ in the body that says, "It's OK. You're safe, and you're *free*." The brain's signal processing sets sexual desire into motion and the body picks up on this cue, which leads to physical arousal. Sex and intimacy for a woman is the major determinant if love is flowing in a relationship.

LOVE IS AN INTOXICANT

How does it feel to be "drunk" in love? Poets and songwriters have written about the intoxicating effects of falling in love. You're intoxicated with each other's presence. That's why falling in love is similar to how you feel after drinking alcohol. It's that same intoxicating feeling that can excite you to the point that your physical and mental control is markedly diminished. It can also cause a wide range of reactions—enthusiasm; frenzy; joy; elation; mental or emotional agitation; disorderly conduct; compulsive activity; and even intense wild, good sex. This is what the easy part of love looks like, but even that by itself is not "love anyway." It too can fade if the ELLER model isn't involved in the process.

The empowerment kind of love is necessary to equip you to experience the hard kind of love—i.e. sharing your feelings, pain, disappointments, and thoughts with your partner—which facilitates sex, the easy kind of love. A thirty-year-old woman is experiencing ELLER; when love flows during the intercourse and orgasm phase of sex. When this happens, the hard part of love and the empowering part of love are flowing. Falling in love has her feeling intoxicated and out of control. The empowerment part of love comes from having an activated spirit.

Of the distinct types of love that date back to ancient Greece culture, let's focus on these three—agape (love for everyone), philieo (loyal and sacrificial love for a friend), and, last but not least, eros (sensual passionate love for someone special). With eros, an orgasm is the height of sensual love, but that pleasurable sensation is only a fraction of love, not love in its totality. To help better understand love, let's also look at what love is and isn't. Love is not a feeling although a part of love is eros love—sex or the easy part of love. Love is action. Love is a choice. Love is serving. Love is giving. Love is making someone feel safe. Love is making someone feel secure. Love is being available for someone. Love is heart-to-heart communication. Love is listening to someone. Love is paying attention to someone. Love is not being codependent. Love is not being controlling. Love is not being demanding.

Empowerment

The ELLER model at its core is all about empowerment. It is the glue that holds all pieces together. Too many relationships are long-lasting but not as enjoyable as when the couple first found love. Then there are couples who have no confidence that their relationship will remain enjoyable or even long-lasting. That's when you'll hear comments like this: "We're doing fine so far. I hope it works out." Does this stem from a lack of empowerment? Instead, why don't we hear, "Whatever comes in our relationship, we're together till death do us part. We will work it through, so love flow continues." Why isn't this claim made more often? Empowerment comes from a spirit-activated heart and causes love to flow. That's why it's crucial that you understand the connection between empowerment and the multiple parts. (See "The Nine-Part Human Theory" chapter.)

The ELLER Model: Building Relationship Practices

Once the spirt is activated, then the ELLER model acts like an X-ray machine going beyond the surface level of issues and problems to begin restoring and building personal and professional relationships. Following the model makes even the most challenging setting becomes easier to navigate. Take a stranger who is predisposed to chatting. The person might ask, "How are you today?" You answer, "Just as good as you." Now, by paying attention to all nine part system of the person's being, you've opened a window into their heart. As people grapple with the implication of the response, there is a "window" that open in their heart. Asking an open-ended question is a noninvasive tool that's part of the ELLER model's toolkit. It quickly begins building a relationship between a forty-two-year-old woman named Beverly and me. Two strangers who, at first, has nothing in common until a window opens. Beverly cordially asks, "So how are you?"

"I am just as good as you," I say, looking right into her eyes.

"Hmmm, that's interesting," she says with a pause.

To put her at ease and deepen the connection, I reply, "Just to let you know, I am a counselor and a writer." Now the more you pay attention in a relationship (at any point), the quicker you can build a relationship from the ground up. I made a conscious decision to be vulnerable with her. I shared my heart with her and, by doing so, set the pace for the rest of our conversation. She has a look on her face that is somewhere between shocked, scared, and intrigued. Relying on the ELLER model, I take the next step to engage her in relational building and communication. Her expression conveys what is on her mind: "What does he know about me?" Observing her choice of words and body language, I start getting "clues" about what is happening in her heart, emotions, and will. She seems to be thinking, *Should I continue this conversation?* Then Beverly let down her guard and says with a thankful smile, "It's like you are looking into my soul." That's how the ELLER model can build relationships after a brief encounter. Imagine what can be accomplished in a session?

WEARING DOWN MEN

Some women think it's their mission. Others grow frustrated and weary from even attempting. The concept of wearing down a man is daunting because it conjures up negative images of a woman nagging, controlling, or chasing down her partner. This approach is exhausting, frustrating, and is no way to alter your partner's behavior. There are five views to explain this behavior: (1) environmental/parental experiences; and upbringing; (2) psychological and physiological influences; and (3) theological impact; (4) Genetic and (5) neurological. Each view has its own complexity and bias. (See appendix for a nonfictional account—"Baffled, Bruised Idiot"—that shows this behavior in action.) So can a woman succeed in wearing down a man? Or better yet, can she influence a man to behavior change? If she is empowered, she can. Empowerment is the cornerstone that supports the ELLER model.

GETTING HELP: TYPES OF COUNSELING

The ELLER model synthesizes the nine part system of every human being and takes a comprehensive, inclusive approach to counseling. The broad field of mental health professionals encompasses those dedicated to helping people with relationship and other issues. Several "parts" of the human being are addressed by members of these groups of professionals. These positions are dedicated to promoting overall mental health—psychiatrist, psychologist, counselors, therapist, sociologist, ministers, pastors, clergy, and social welfare workers. All of these professional titles are partitioned and exclusive. For example, ministers, pastors, and Christian psychologists tend to focus on the heart, spirit, mind, and will. Psychologists, social workers, sociologists, therapists, and counselors turn their attention to the cognitive—the mind, and emotions. For example, psychiatrists are included in this group to promote wellness and prescribe medication for severe behavior issues. The ELLER Model takes a comprehensive inclusive approach to counseling undergirded by understanding of Love and Empowerment.

The ELLER Model Frequently Asked Questions

1. *Are there some marriages that will never benefit from the ELLER model and destined for divorce?*

   All marriages can put the ELLER model into practice. Based on the nine-part human theory, an activated spirit in the heart by at least one person in the marriage is all that's needed. This gives one or both partners empowerment to influence the other person's behavior. There are no marriages that can't benefit from this model. In fact, working closely with ELLER coaches, the model can change a 90 percent man under the influence of a 90 percent woman. Conversely, a 10 percent man can influence a 10 percent woman and save their marriage. Also, a 90 percent woman can influence a 90 percent man and rebuild their relationship and restore their marriage.

2. *Does a someone special, the one and only, really exist for every person?*

   Unless you are given the power to be celibate, finding love perfectly and that special person is possible (See Appendix for nonfictional story, "Die or I Will Kill You," based on a real-life counseling session.) Find that person whose 9 parts has their spirit activated and captivate them with your beauty. Let's say you're a 90% woman, then influence your 90% man down to a 10% man. Now you will know as the empowerment and the influence works that you are finding love perfectly, and that's the special someone. The people who give up on finding that special someone lack the knowledge of the ELLER model.

3. *Why does it seem as if a wife is more involved than her husband in incorporating the model into their marriage?*

A 90 percent woman (and 10 percent man) are the ones who influence and are empowered to save their marriage. It's the same reason there are a higher percentage of women serving in churches, synagogues, temples, and other places where the heart is exhibited. It's common that 90 percent of women speak straight from their hearts and feelings more than 90 percent of men. There is no logical reason why this phenomenon happens. No "ology" (psychology, physiology, sociology, etc.) can explain this. The only place left to look is theology or the spirit. In order to get the answer, you would have to shut off your mind temporarily, and the spirit will help you from there.

4. *Why don't men open up?*

It seems that 90 percent men don't open up. A 90 percent woman whose husband is a CEO of a major company (one-million-dollar annual salary with perks) asked that same question. She has everything that money can buy—expensive houses, multiple credit cards, dream vacations, and endless spending money. Every woman's dream, right? Wrong. She does not have his heart because he doesn't open up and share his heart with her. In the workplace, he's an outstanding executive and communicator but shuts down at home or tries to manage her heart with the same tools he uses with employees. It just doesn't work like that! Is this wife experiencing the ELLER model? When approached by an ELLER coach, she was like a starving woman desperately begging for crumbs. Ninety percent of women can influence 90 percent men to open up because they are empowered and have the activated spirit in their heart. The tool in the model to do this is asking open questions in a noninvasive way with persistence. Love is the tool she's using to change her approach with her husband. When you can answer the question, What's love anyway? you realize that love is a most powerful tool in your toolkit. Over time, most 90 percent men will soften up and, realize that you love them, and eventually share their heart.

A young thirty-year-old wife had a similar relationship issue with her spouse. She explains, "He is fine in every way, but I just can't get him to open up even when we engage in good sex." There is no logical answer. Sitting on a bookshelf is a more than two-hundred-page book titled, *What Men Know about Women*. When a man opens the book, every page is blank. For 90 percent men, communicating with their wife or girlfriend is like staring at a blank page. An empowered woman who understands the ELLER model not only knows why but also knows how to get 90 percent men to open up. Another book written by a male psychologist and a sociologist tackled the same issue. Again, there are no substantive answer or solution.

5. *Why do wives lose interest in sex?*

As many women age, they progressively lose interest in the sex, the easy part of love. But loss of sexual desire can happen at any age due to physiology or hormonal changes. But many married women are affected by the 90 percent man in their life. These women eventually become 10 percent women who are divorced and emotionally damaged.

Working together, the nine-part human theory and activated spirit in their heart can change this situation. A 10 percent man who is empowered and has an activated spirit in his heart can cause his partner to maintain her desire and engage in sex with him. There are three parts of love that makes ELLER and love flow and keep love flowing. (1) The empowering part of love; (2) the hard part of love; and (3) the easy part of love—sex. The empowering part of love (the activated spirit in the heart) equips the woman to experience and do the hard part of love (i.e., heart-to-heart communication—open up, share, be vulnerable—and the hard part of love facilitates the easy part of love. Every woman will tell you that. Just about all affairs, divorces, and love, not flowing situations are due to the three types of love not synchronizing together as seen in the RDC curve. This is a proven rationale as to why women lose desire in the easy part of love.

6. *Why do men almost never lose interest in sex?*

Some women think men never lose interest in sex. I wish the answer were that simple, but it isn't. Men are aroused by visual images—women's legs, breasts, and butt (See Appendix, nonfictional story "Baffled, Bruised Idiot" based on my counseling experiences). And 90 percent men are clueless when it comes to matters of love and being vulnerable. This is the same reason why you find fewer men in churches, synagogues, temples—places where the opening up of the heart or the hard things happen.

This is an issue with women when love is not flowing but can be corrected by empowerment, activated spirit in the heart, and influence. The visual problem of lust can only be controlled by an activated spirit and empowerment. Women don't want to be objectified. Ninety percent men can be transformed in this area through empowerment, influence, and the activated spirit in the heart so they can keep the interest in sex balanced and their wives/girlfriends can maintain their sexual desire within their committed relationship.

7. *Why do men struggle with erection problems?*

Men struggle with erection problems causing their wives to be dissatisfied sexually. Putting aside the physiological reasons, which can be medically corrected, the psychological reasons are locked within the secret of the nine-part human theory. Marriage therapists encourage and challenge couples to spend a minute together touching. Greeting each other with a hug after work each day can lead to erection and vaginal stimulation. The heart eventually is stimulated. The mind is influenced. The will and emotions are engaged given the time and attention beyond three minutes, continuous kissing (which is skin-on-skin touching that engages the brain and releases hormones into the blood flow). Suddenly, the heart beats faster and pumps the blood to the penis. The result is an erection, and then nature takes over. So a huge part of erection problem is the fact that love is not flowing. The woman isn't excited because her husband is not incorporating the three kinds of love that the ELLER model emphasizes. (See "The ELLER Model" chapter.)

A forty-year-old wife (90 percent woman) is married to a fifty-year-old husband (90 percent man) has a low desire for sex but loves sex. Go figure! Her husband is not managing her heart well and doesn't know how to ask open, noninvasive questions. That sets off a chain reaction of events: his wife is not excited; hormones aren't released; and her will is not ready. She really doesn't want to have sex with her husband because her vagina is not lubricated. The result—a weak erection, dissatisfying sex, and no ELLER. After a frustrating six weeks without sex and love flow diminishes. This leaves the function of the mind, anxiety, emotion, fear, worry, and lack of confidence contributing heavily to their overall dissatisfaction. The ELLER model, along with its coaches, can change erection problems.

8. *How does a wife enjoy sex when she only sees it as a duty, an obligation, or when she's not in the mood?*

A wife can enjoy sex by using the ELLER model and enlist an ELLER coach. It is virtually impossible for a wife to enjoy sex and, in many cases, to agree to sex when there is a damaged human heart due to her 90 percent husband's hurtful words and actions. No sharing from the heart or resolving conflicts can kill the mood. The break in their deadlock starts with the ELLER model and leads to heart-to-heart communication facilitated by an ELLER coach, if necessary. Marcy, thirty-two, is a 90 percent woman whose husband is a typical 90 percent husband unable to open up. Silence then leads to the couple sweeping their unresolved conflicts and issues under the rug. The result—build-up of emotional pain. Meeting with an ELLER coach prompts change and activates the spirit in both their hearts. Over a period of time, honest and intimate communication can only improve with the ELLER coaching. Marcy later confessed that the ELLER coaching resulted in the best sex she has ever experienced. Now sex is no longer a duty but pleasurable and she connects now with her husband.

9. *Would the ELLER model ever advise someone to dissolve their marriage and get a divorce?*

ELLER would *never* advise a couple to stop working on their marriage. The empowerment aspect of our model wouldn't allow it. Quitting is a function of the mind, emotion, body, and will only. When the heart and activated spirit are involved, there is empowerment. ELLER coaching can provide the support, encouragement, teaching, comfort, and advice that both husband and wife need to make Love Flow.

10. *Are verbal, emotional, or physical abuses ground for divorce?*

Call 911 if you are being physically abused. Verbal abuse and emotional abuse may not always be grounds for divorce. Instead, it is grounds for seeking ELLER coaching and restoring your relationship. Too many couples use emotional and verbal abuses as an excuse for divorce because they don't want to go through the pain of working on their love and relationship. Couples want the gain but not pain. The ELLER model reinforces that where there is pain, there is greater gain.

11. *Can the ELLER model operate without the three parts of love?*

Empowerment, the hard part of love, and the easy part of love, are essential to the model.

12. *Why is sex such a struggle in marriage?*

Many couples fail to realize that sex isn't a free ride. It takes empowerment and the hard part of love to make sex work. Too many people don't want to pay the price to make sex work in their relationship and marriage. Do the pain, get the gain.

13. *How do I get my man to open up?*

By loving and supporting him. Ask open questions noninvasively with persistence to help him get to the heart of the matter. It takes an activated spirit to have the patience, gentleness, and controlled emotions to get a man to open up.

14. *Why don't women frequently climax during sex?*

Women are not always stimulated—mentally, emotionally, and physically—by their man (See appendix for nonfictional story "Deafening Cry" taken from my actual counseling cases.) Emotional foreplay is a heart-to-heart connection that can lead to the hard part of love. This then leads to physical foreplay (the skin theory), and then sexual intercourse can lead to climax. For a woman, climaxing is more than physical; whereas for a man, the physical is often sufficient.

15. *Why do women/wives avoid having sex?*

This is a deep and complex question. Some women say it is because they are not in the mood. They don't feel like it. They're simply not into it. Because you've been ugly! They are not treated right (See Appendix for nonfictional story "Deafening Cry.") There is the way that the ELLER model asks to get into their heart and truly understand why women avoid sex, even sabotaging the possibility of sex happening. Most men don't even ask a woman why she doesn't want to have sex, which compounds the problem. The woman who is gradually drifting from a 90 percent woman (or closer to a 10 percent woman due to a damaged heart) also compounds the problem by not opening up as to why she is avoiding sex. Instead, she pronounces blame on her partner as opposed to honesty speaking her mind. The ways women choose to sabotage or avoid sex further shows the need for the ELLER model—sleeping on the couch as opposed to with her partner, going to bed after her husband is asleep, dressing unattractively on purpose, and avoiding intimacy instead. To put it simply, their body is unprepared for sex because of a number of complex factors: (1) The hard part of love—not talking with the mouth. Heart-to-heart communication is not happening either by the wife or husband; (2) the empowerment part of love is not being expressed by the woman; (3) hardening her heart; (4) unforgiveness keeps your heart closed; and the brain is not getting any signals to prepare the body, vagina, and mind to anticipate sex. The skin is not experiencing arousal. No kissing, foreplay, fondling, caressing, cuddling is happening. The will isn't invoked. In short, the nine-part human theory shuts down.

Sabotaging made Peggy dress plainly every day and let herself go. She stops wearing makeup and getting her hair and nails done. And of course, no negligees worn to bed. Then one day, she dresses up royally for a doctor's appointment. She has gotten tired of being a plain Jane. She has worn lipstick, perfume, and a skintight blouse; and has her hair done. Her husband goes berserk and, in a rage, accuses her of an affair. Even after a hard day at work or at home with the kids, some women will still find a way to put on perfume and wear a seductive dress to greet her husband as he comes home from work. That is the opposite of avoiding.

The ELLER model keeps a couple's behavior on track, reinforces the importance of empowerment, and shows them how to manage their hearts.

16. *Can chemical imbalance be cured?*

Chemical imbalance is a frequently diagnosed emotional behavior problem affecting relationships. Medication is the most frequent way of addressing chemical imbalance, which is a function of the brain. Science using technology has proven that there is an imbalance of chemicals in the brain that accounts for some behavior problems. How can this imbalance be corrected? Can science balance this imbalance? When a psychiatrist or neurologist determines a chemical imbalance, the remedy is medication that neutralizes and modifies the particular behavior. Medication does not cure a chemical imbalance or have the empowerment to change behavior. The ELLER model recommends this first rule of approach: address the brain-related behavior instead of going directly to the brain physiological approach. In addition, incorporate the nine-part human theory and explore the empowerment of the spirit in the heart. Medication can help chemical imbalance and soothe the behavior problem but may not complete fix it, heal, or and change the person's behavior.

17. *Where does the conscience fit, and can it be changed?*

People looking for relationships behave in a way that seems as if they lack conscience. Selfishness is one of the byproducts when there appears someone is functioning without any conscience. You can have a great mind (summa cum laude, MIT genius, PhD) but without any conscience. You look attractive like a runway model and still behave as if you don't have a conscience. Conscience is not related to emotion, mind, body, skin, mouth, or will. The answer is related to the heart and the spirit. Conscience is related to the heart. A person can find love from the heart, but there's no guarantee. Statistics show that a couple might still end up in divorce. The conscience is in need of a fix. The activated spirit resident in the heart is the answer. An activated spirit in the heart gives the empowerment to fix the conscience, alter the heart, and improve love flow.

18. *Is the ELLER model more effective than dating apps and online dating services? How does it compare?*

Can these dating apps and online services peer into people's heart and mind to determine if their spirits are activated? That's what our model does and so much more. Understanding the degree of damage there's been to a person's heart is instrumental in matching them with a compatible partner. These data points would be helpful in finding love perfectly—their home environment when growing up, how their parents modeled love, impact of separation or divorce on the home, their own love life, stable or turbulent relationships, or indulging in affairs.

Appendices

Stories Based on the ELLER Model

NIGHTMARE IN A CRATER

Nadia's stature may have been short, but she was long on extroversion, charm, and controversy. She had long wrestled with her height and who she was, even though others saw she had what it takes. She woke up in the village wrestling with her nightmarish dream wondering if her experience was dream or reality. Her life seemed to be one of discovery. Finding out about others while not wanting others to find out about her was who she was. As a student of anthropology, the village was the right place to be.

It was anyone's guess as to the village's origin. Even its inhabitants were curious. The only ones who were not curious were AN4 and CG5. The village was a place etched out as a crater where five hundred people could easily live. It was years before the inhabitants of this northernmost part of Siberia had known about the strange crater.

Consequently, there was enough time for AN4 and CG5, the original residents of the village, to get to know the area. AN4 was five feet four inches tall with a professor look, bow tie and glasses to match. CG5's beauty was Polynesian with many cultures combined. She was proper in dress and decorum. It was widely believed that AN4 and CG5 came from outer space on the object that created the crater. Nobody really knew. Nadia was at the village desperately wanting to discover about other cultures, even as she resisted her own discovery. On the other hand, AN4 and CG5 resisted discovery, but they had wisdom beyond earthlings.

The sun was coming up as Nadia headed to the village community center to meet AN4 and CG5 for the weekly "culturerama"—a time to get to know one another. Bubbly and gleefully, she greeted them. "Why are your names different from mine?" she said. "And what does the 4 and 5 stand for?"

With rapid speech and no pause, Nadia said, "Were you orbited out or sent from outer space?" They intentionally did not answer even though they were quite able to communicate.

AN4 began to try to get to know her too. His way seemed to be more indirect and in-depth, reaching the heart and with no verbal communication. Nadia was beginning to enquire what communication really means in its universal heartfelt sense. The mystery on top of mystery was beginning to be much for Nadia's extroverted, controlling personality. "Good morning, AN4, how are you?" she greeted again, trying a different approach.

AN4 replied, "Just as good as you."

What kind of answer is that? Nadia mused to herself. She was no more aware as to how he was, as she began to look inward at what she was doing wrong.

It seemed like it was a game to AN4, but was it? She started to think out loud that the *4* in his name maybe meant the four traits of listening, so important to discovery. Somewhere she had heard that. So far, sharing, listening, and responding were not happening. Such an important part of getting to know someone. Despite her efforts, it seemed he wanted to know how she was doing also or maybe even getting to know her. Nadia said to AN, as he liked to be called, "You did not answer my question." With her charming smile aglow, she was compelling as she pressed into what she thought was his heart.

AN said to her, "Guess what?" She waited with baited breath for the completion of the sentence. Sometimes that preface meant something else would be said. No other words from AN. She hated surprises, guessing, and playing games. She liked things to be straightforward and quick. "This culturerama is getting to me," she muttered to herself. AN was waiting for her to open up. In the meantime, CG5 was not saying much but would give eye contact to AN and affirm that she was paying attention and giving moral support. They seemed to know each other very well.

In the midst of Nadia's frustration, she said, "When challenge is pursued persistently, there is discovery." Nadia helped herself from getting frustratingly mad and shouted, "I am done!" her usual signal when charm was not working.

Nadia recognized AN's persistence and effort in trying to get to know her by opening up. Nadia heard him say, "What is going on?" More open questions, designed to get her to open up her heart were asked. Nadia's hands flew into the air in disgust.

This day was coming to an end, and Nadia's nightmare was over like a pot boiling over and steam coming out until you could see the bottom of the pot. Nadia bit her lip as she walked back and forth and talked in short sentences and broken sentences. She began to open up to AN. She said, "I get it, AN! I can see where opening up to you will help me feel better about myself." She spent the next hour sharing about her own life.

She sat back with an awkward smile, awake and knowing AN better, knowing herself better too and discovering who she really was. Being discovered, she realized, was like being at the bottom of the pot. This smile was different from her norm. She thought, *Dream or reality, a discovery took place in me today.* "I feel better about myself," she said. "I allowed myself to be known. It was good to wake up to such a reality." I went to discover and was discovered.

DEAFENING CRY

To Kelly, reaching thirty was like being 10,800 days old with a biological clock ticking so loud it was deafening. A journalist, she sat in the sub-Sahara office of Dr. Ted Balir waiting for him to arrive and thinking intermittently about the man who her friends speculated was imaginary. Her legs were shaking back and forth with rhythmic speed like a grandfather clock going *tick, tock, tick, tock*. Back in Southern Illinois, she would have been in a deep sleep at this time of day. Her jet lag rocked the chair as she kept trying to sit straight. She wondered what Dr. Blair would think if he came in right now. Her mind was not cooperating with her tired body; all she could recall was her friends saying she was traveling to escape from something. Some say she was traveling to find something.

She was aware of her beauty. She stood six feet tall with hips like a Maasai Mara queen. She could walk looking like a model going down the runway. Her brown eyes captivated you even if she was only on the cover of *Cosmopolitan*. Her swaying hips were enough to make any boyfriend or a husband's jaw drop.

The sting of the twelfth relationship breakup was the messiest; it was like a bad anniversary and still raw. This date, August 2010, brought back bad memories. The previous eleven relationship dumps were her doing, but Tony was the one who dumped this time. Her looks didn't seem to be helping her any. Travel, work, anything to help ease the pain, would do. She asked her boss Frank for an assignment to do a story on the cold Kinter case, and he gladly granted it to her.

Finally, the door cracked, and Dr. Blair walked in, reminding her of the noise she heard when Tony came to her apartment on that fateful night. Her mind raced, and she teared up.

"Hello there, you must be Kelly, how are you?" Dr. Blair said, trying to make eye contact. She didn't want him to see her tears, so she stared down at the floor. Her image of him was like the other men in her life. "Your boss, he went on, who is a personal friend of mine, told me you might benefit from being part of my seminar on sex, the easy part of love."

Is he kidding? she thought. Sex was about the last thing she wanted to even remotely think about, much less talk about. The feeling it invoked stabbed her as she sat there without an answer.

"This might help the Kinter case," Dr. Blair went on, "because the seminar takes a look at sex and the role the heart plays regarding sex, the emotional heart, that is."

"What do you mean by that?" Kelly said.

"The heart sends messages to all parts of your body in the sex experience of love flow," said Dr. Blair.

Hmmm! Kelly said to herself.

She was intrigued by the heart approach.

"OK!" she said, "sounds interesting!" She thought of Dr. Balir as a bush doctor from the dark interior of Africa. His safari-type jacket, khaki shorts, and sandals, his penetrating eyes, fit the part even though he was an African-born, London-trained psychologist.

"See you tomorrow at 9:00 a.m. upstairs in room 305," he said.

During a short taxi ride to downtown Tabora, the taxi driver, inadvertently mentioned the name Kinter, and Kelly took a deep sigh. The taxi pulled up at her hotel, and she went in the lobby, sat, and opened up the envelope with the details of the Kinter case. It read, "Playboy-type African man freed of murder rape charge, escapes, now misunderstood." The thoughts of her troubles, the victim's heart and similar sexual experiences enraged her into palpitations.

She sat there drinking a cup of tea and reflecting on the case and some similarities to what Dr. Blair had said about the seminar before going upstairs to bed.

Oh no! she thought. Not about a lover, murder, sex mystery. Kinter's picture brought a feeling of disgust to her. His eyes had this sinister look. Maria Gonzales was a white thirty-year-old stripper who had vanished and later found raped and mutilated with a tattoo on her groin.

*****

The night passed, and Kelly arrived in room 305 at 9:00 a.m. There were six women and five men sitting around in a circle; Dr. Blair in his khaki shorts and a safari jacket was also sitting in the circle. *I hate this!* she thought with a snicker. His opening remarks were, "The heart is the control tower of every part of the body." The task was for that concept to be discussed as he moderated. Kelly thought that the comment was as huge as the three-story building they were in and as deep as the Pacific Ocean near by Dar Salem. Kelly's heart raced as the session started; her body felt like she was in a straight-jacket. Up to this point, her journal was the only way she expressed her flawed feelings. She was expecting more of a lecture given the sheltered life she experienced growing up. She sat next to Ube, this pretty black woman.

Ube was the first one to share. She was a thirty-one-year-old African native who had several breakups. She'd been healed through Dr. Blair's seminars. She was currently in a great relationship and engaged to be married. Her Creole accent mixed with British slipped out as she said with a broad smile, "My heart controls my body in my relationship now." Kelly thought, *Why is she here? She seemed like a plant, like she understood what he was saying. Everyone else seemed to be looking for an answer.*

Kelly turned instinctively and looked at Ube. *What does she know that I don't?*

The men in the circle were very quiet, all except one who said, "What does the heart have to do with sex?"

What an idiot! Kelly thought. She knew there was a connection somehow. The man reminded her of Ken, someone she had dated. She briefly stared out the window and cracked her knuckles. Maybe a lot of men don't have a clue about the heart and sex connection. *Giving Ken my body, my heart, my soul … what a waste.* She stared out the window and cracked her knuckles again.

Dr. Blair sat there observing and listening as though taking mental notes.

Kelly was beginning to see that there was much more to the subject. She felt some voids filling up in her like empty canisters being filled up by the falling rain. She didn't feel as dry as when she came into the circle.

Dr. Blair interjected, "Sharing, listening and responding between couples makes for a heart connection."

Ube nodded her head and looked straight at Kelly. She said, "Many people don't understand this concept I call it the ELLLER Model Concept (Experiencing Long Lasting and Enjoyable Relationship). You can tell from the blank stares coming from the other men and women in the group." Ube continued to explain, "Like Dr. Blair said, the heart is like a control tower. If all is right within the heart of a woman, it gives the green light to all other areas of the body."

The confused look on Kelly's faced prompted Ube to give an example from her own life. She continued, "In my relationship, when I feel my heart is really known by my boyfriend, my desire for him intensifies."

Back in the session, another man made a wisecrack about sex, and the conversation started to veer in another direction. Kelly was annoyed. Men were so clueless, she said! Was it any wonder some relationships don't work!

Interest already piqued, Kelly was distant for the rest of the session as Ube's words sank in and were pondered. She was intent on finding out more about this heart connection when she could catch Ube alone.

Kelly snapped back into the present moment when she heard the squeak of the chairs as people got up for the break. She turned to find Ube walking up the aisle toward the lobby. She followed her out the door to get her attention.

"Excuse me," Kelly blurted. "Do you have a moment so we can talk?"

"Of course, hon, let's sit down over here."

Ube led Kelly to a comfy couch in a small hall off the main lobby. Kelly's anxiety rose. Speaking to a complete stranger about something as intimate as relationships was foreign to her, but her desperate need to know trumped her fear. As they sat, Ube's warm smile somehow melted the pang out of her anxiety and gently put her more at ease. Ube spoke first, "What can I do for you, hon?" Her compassion was genuine.

Kelly could feel it, so she answered, "I ... I want to know more ... what did you mean by 'knowing the heart'?"

Ube leaned forward. "When the heart of a woman is satisfied, it's known, heard, and understood, and then it frees her up."

"But how does a man do all that for her?"

Ube went on, "To know anyone, you have to spend *time* with them and ask a lot of questions. Questions will prompt a woman to share the things in her heart when she feels her man is asking because he is genuine in his compassion and intently listening. Knowing each other means knowing each other's struggles, weaknesses, pain, and passion. Do you see the vulnerability? When a woman feels safe enough and listened to in order to open up like that, she can turn around and make that man a happy man!"

Thoughts of past relationships suddenly fired off in Kelly's head. Did those guys really take the time to know her? She couldn't remember a single relationship in which she felt treasured. All conversations seemed so superficial with one goal in mind.

"It's all physiological, hon," Ube was saying, "When the heart connection is made, the freed heart sends a message to every part of the body, starting with the brain. Hormones are sent rushing into her system, her heart pumps the hormones throughout, and her interest for intimacy is ignited."

"That's the connection!" Kelly said out loud. The dots suddenly connected!

"So, all this superficial stuff is like giving your heart away cheaply, right?"

"Yes!" replied Ube with a huge grin as she realized Kelly had caught on. "Most men don't care about the heart stuff as much as they should and need to. Intimacy for a woman starts with her heart. If more men caught onto that, their women would be so much more receptive."

Kelly thought about all the times in her past and how exciting "love" was at first until her desires started to wane. "Can I ask you something personal?" she said, looking straight into Ube's brown eyes. Ube's warm look accompanied her nod, and Kelly continued, "Did you ever lose desire in your relationships?"

"Yes, eventually my heart sensed that he didn't care, and I began losing interest in him. He sensed that, and his behavior toward me changed. The rest is history—break up!"

Kelly cringed as she thought of the similarities. After the break, as eleven people interacted, this turned on light bulbs inside of Kelly. She was beginning to feel relieved. She thought of how shallow her relationships had been, and with a deep sigh of relief, she left the session.

*****

Kelly tossed and turned all night thinking about her heart as she was beginning to get in touch with it. She was starting to have strangely renewed feelings in her body.

Her contact told her Kinter had left Tabora for Jamaica. Kelly immediately made arrangements for a flight out to Jamaica.

Suddenly, the phone rang. It was Ube.

"Can I meet you to talk more?"

"I am headed to Jamaica," Kelly told her.

"May I come with you? I find your story fascinating, and the timing would fit nicely for a vacation."

"Absolutely!" Kelly said.

The flight from Dar Salem, Tanzania, was on Air Jamaica. On the tail wing, two large flamingos almost blended into each other. The words below them said, "Lovebirds." Kelly was so bewildered as to why that couldn't be her reality. She wanted her heart blended in all twelve relationships. This was a symbol of two hearts blended together. *Heart, lovebirds, hmmm!* She wished that this blending had happened.

The Jetway into the plane was filled with reggae sounds that seemed to move her to a different place. "This is feeling more like a vacation," Kelly blurted out. With Ube tagged along, Kelly looked forward to meeting Kinter, getting a story, and getting to know Ube better.

The greeting at the top of stairs was, "Welcome to Air Jamaica."

"Maybe I should just move there," she said lightheartedly, and she reclined in her seat with a Jamaica punch. The boisterous need for love continued to stir within her as she buckled in and closed her eyes shut for a minute.

*****

Once again, the hot tropical breeze of ninety-degree weather welcomed her in Jamaica. The feeling of being in there with someone she was getting to know was a stark contrast from Tanzania.

A festival was on in upper Kingston, and Kelly and Ube went to unwind before working on the Kinter case. Kelly was continuing to connect the dots in her heart as she headed to the festival. Sex, communication, heart. Twelve agonizing crying sessions for the combination of love had made her almost deaf. Kelly felt like a meltdown was clearing the wax in her ear that had deafened her.

Looking at Ube squarely, she said, "I don't need to be deaf anymore. I don't have to cry for love because I am learning to know what to look for now."

"Sounds good to me," Ube said with a smile.

Kelly arrived with Ube at 6:00 p.m. to a huge park in upper Barbican. There was music, food and people everywhere, like Bourbon Street in New Orleans.

Suddenly, a familiar figure walked up to them.

"Holy smokes!" Kelly said. There is Kinter coming straight at us. She recognized him from the pictures. Her knees were shaking, and her stomach rumbling just at the sight of him. Every fiber in her being shook. Kelly knew she had to tap into her new learning to get into his heart and understand the case.

He walked up to them. "My name is Kinter," he said. "Can I buy you a drink?" He was looking straight at Kelly.

"Sure!" Kelly said with an investigative boldness and disgust.

Ube kept quiet knowing more about African and Jamaican men. But the theories of the heart, body, sex, mouth come rushing back to Kelly's mind like a flood. Not only was she investigating what he was accused of doing, but now she was more curious as to why he was accused.

"I will take the drink if you will share your heart with me," Kelly said quietly. Kinter was not used to a woman who appeared to be empowered. Calling the shots, that was his role.

I can't believe this is me! Kelly thought.

The anger inside of Kinter started to surface as he bit his upper lip.

"I can understand why the anger and why you hesitate to share your heart," Kelly said.

"What do you care, white girl?" Kinter lashed out his anger overflowing from within.

"But Kelly stared right into his dark eyes and whispered, "I know you are hurting."

"This ain't worth it. I am outta here," Kinter said.

He turned to escape the uncomfortable conversation, but Kelly boldly grabbed his arm. The fierce rage and surprise that Kelly clearly read on his face startled her for a moment.

"Are you going to run again?" she pursued gently.

"Look, man, you don't know *nothin*! All of you are the same."

A pregnant paused filled the air.

"Who hurt you?" Kelly asked once again.

"Kinter's rage-filled face turned away. He was stunned! His male emotional barrier was shattered like glass while his eyes filled with tears, and torrents of words evoked.

The understanding of Kinter's heart was like a triathlon. He felt understood. Her story to the paper on *Understanding the Heart* led to the pursuit of the real killer, and Kelly got to confirm to herself that she knew how to really find love Perfectly and experience ELLER.

DIE OR I WILL KILL YOU

Nirma rolled over to a cold space and woke up at 3:00 a.m. on the dot. Tears dripped from her big brown Eskimo eyes. This had been her worst sexual experience; it hurt even in her damn dreams. She hauled the covers over her head with hate for her life but with a goal of healing and a future.

It was 7:00 a.m. Monday, Bloomington, Alaska time, and Nirma sat on the bed with her legs crossed and her hands on her jaw. Today was a new day for her at age twenty-six. The empty house after college and ROTC and the waiting for assignment in the Army was a constant reminder of the emptiness she felt inside. The pain of the seven-hundred-dollar sexual threesome from those executives blasted her like dynamite. *Well, I needed the money for tuition,* she thought. The killing and dying thesis that she just completed gnawed at her like a buzz saw. Her symbolic way of looking at things pervaded her thinking. "Die or I will kill you" was a prime example.

In Bloomington, you could see the polar bears and icebergs. Coast guard cutters made their way through the ice, and that was fun for the kids riding around on dog drawn sleds. While growing up there, Nirma's mom made money the sleazy way. It felt like she was being molested just watching her mom. Dad died when she was two years old. Hanging around the Army base was everything to her. Nirma was the lonely soldier's plaything. Nobody did put her first, only themselves. She would kill for someone to do that.

Nirma left home for six years, desperate and with a goal to heal, fulfill her dream for college, and to find love. She got her master's degree from University of Washington in nursing, cum laude. Her fascinating thesis was about how the Army allowed captured insurgents to die and about the relationship between killing and dying. All this was possible while she marched the sleazy Seattle streets.

She loved her five-foot five-inch frame. She was twenty-years-old, but she felt like a sixteen-year-old. Her cheeks and her walk was pronounced, and her smile baited all the executive high tippers. They were drawn to her like trapped mice that kept coming back. She knew there was simply no one on Brown Street like her, but she hated every minute of it. She wondered what the real thing felt like and hated herself getting sucked into mom's lifestyle.

*****

The phone call for Army assignment had lifted her spirits toward new life. It was the winter and drill preparation time. Nirma had enlisted as a lieutenant and Army nurse. Colonel Kime was the leader of her unit. The blustering wind on this cold morning was not her only distraction. She saw uniform, and her heart saw leader. Her mind raced as Kime spoke. She saw him beyond the leader way down to a safety net. She shook her body and tightened her vest and thought, *What would I do for some of that live blanket.* Kime was a fascination of hers, Rom, and other Eskimo soldiers. Kime was this tall, good-looking black dude who rose from being an alcoholic in the Washington, DC, ghetto to make full-bird colonel. His voice was like the guy in the Allstate insurance ad: "You are in good hands with Allstate." He spoke and you felt you were in good hands, the kind Nirma had been searching for.

The next day, it was time to go to Afghanistan. She climbed into the giant, C5 almost forgetting one of her bags. The steady wooing of the large engines was interrupted by the giant bird dropping what felt like a mile. Nirma clutched her chest and reached for her airbag, "Yuk!" Everyone else seemed to be sleeping but her, but sleep might bring her dream back. She wished Kime was in the back of the plane to hold her. Her thoughts swaggered from marching days to her thesis and to what she was about to face. These insurgents would kill anything American, and her job was to save them from dying.

Twenty hours must have passed by. The C5 bumped on the tarmac. There was bright sunlight and noises strange to Bloomington. There were mountains on all sides. Camp Kandahar was tucked in a valley near the Pakistan border. She tightened her shoulders and walked toward the door. The rocket propelled missiles feinted against the F15 fighter jets that roared above. The *ratatat* of a AK-7 was the norm. Meanwhile the breathtaking valleys and glacier-topped mountains with caves looked down. It was like perfume on top of a landfill.

*****

The gun battle that next day was her welcome, and Brinka was the wounded insurgent bleeding to death. She still had her veil on; she insisted. Her face was hardy as a man.

"I don't want to die," Brinka said in her broken English.

Nirma steadied her hands as she treated her. She remembered her thesis and sighed. Thoughts of dying relating to killing came flooding into her head. Brinka had no idea what was going on in Nirma's head.

"I understand your desperation," Nirma said. Her hands trembled and beads of sweat started down her face.

"How could you?" Brinka said.

Her thesis and research showed that the US Army personnel would let a captured wounded insurgent die without effort to save them. The rules of engagement were clear. This was more like killing to her. Nirma held her as she bandaged her wound. She looked away briefly and sniffled.

Throughout her life, Nirma's compassion for suffering pushed her to do things. Going into the military seemed to be more complex, though; so was her thesis. Maybe this military was an escape. She needed to talk to Kime about these thoughts and feelings. She stood there shaking her head after the treatment.

She went to his office the next day, and thoughts raced back to the preparation day.

"I need to talk to you," she said. She held her stomach tightly as he looked up. Kime just looked at her like a leader. Just what she wanted. She sat down and crossed her leg. The war that was waging inside her was worse than the war with the Taliban.

"What is this about?" said Kime.

"Thoughts and feelings of killing and dying while treating Brinka, the prisoner," Nirma told him.

"Do you have feelings for this killer?" asked Kime.

She looked away. *I have feelings for you,* she said to herself.

"Are you okay?" Kime said, asking her a second question.

Nirma just smiled. Just what she wanted to hear. A strong man comforting her and getting into her heart. Just then, she looked him square in the eyes sternly and said, "I hope you aren't thinking that I am incompetent to handle my job. I am fine now."

"Okay, dismissed, soldier," said Kime.

She watched him walk away, shrugging his shoulders.

Camp Kandahar was no place to chitchat, but there were several wars raging inside of Nirma, and she hoped inside of Kime too. Nirma suggested they chat further.

*****

Time opened up that Thursday evening, and Nirma approached Kime in the officer's lounge. The stars, the elevation, and the snow-capped mountain were a perfect scene for romance with the any-time threat of an attack. The smell of gunpowder and rocket fuel was like perfume to Nirma. The conversation in the tent got off war and focused elsewhere.

Kime spoke first. "As your commanding officer, I have access to your files and knowledge of your background," he said.

Where is he going with that? Nirma wondered as she twiddled her thumbs. She loved the focus being put on her and not on him. A part of her wanted to trust and let go, the part she was trying to conceal from him. It was like a tug-o-war.

"I want to get to know you," Kime said.

"What don't you know that you want to know?" she asked. She leaned back bracing, almost tilting her chair.

"The files dealt with facts, but I want to hear what you have to say. I want to know you, that's more important to me. Washington State University and I understand working your way up through university, but this thesis 'Die or I Will Kill You,' I don't understand."

Nirma cringed! "No one has ever asked me that before," she said. Tears started to flow.

"Tears of joy or tears of sadness?" Kime said, eyeballing her, knowing he connected with the bulls-eye and maybe even the symbolic and literal meaning behind the thesis.

"Nirma shut the tears off quickly after giving Kime a glimpse of her heart and again stared out the window. The moment was like an avalanche heading straight to her heart door barricaded for twenty-six years. Kime held her hands gently, looking in her big eyes and said nothing. No words out of Nirma's mouth either, but more tears.

Kime was an interrogator with the CIA before his promotion, and he was using it with icing on top.

*****

The curfew on the officer's club was drawing to a close. The avalanche was getting closer and closer. *I can't give in to this so quickly or I am dead meat*, Nirma thought as she started to feel unglued inside. But she wanted to so badly. Any man could take her away now. She tightened her jaws. She glanced outside at the stars and thought, *This feels like heaven, but I must think symbolic.* It was the easiest thing she knew how to do, just like marching, taking care of men while none of them took care of her. Nirma sat up straight in her chair and grasped her hands.

"Tell me about yourself," she asked.

"It has been a journey to get to where I am in life. I have never found love, but I like what I am feeling right now," said Kime.

"What's that?" Nirma asked.

"You!"

Nirma cracked a smile.

It was curfew time again. A short walk to her tent and she was lying in bed turning from side to side. She got up, checked Facebook, voice mail, Twitter, e-mail, and text. The very thing that could calm her down was left behind. Then she turned on her iTunes and plugged her ears to Etta James belting out in melodious tone, "At last my love has come along / My lonely days are over and life is like a song." She shivered! All nine part system of her were in motion—skin, heart, emotion, body, brain, mind, spirit, even the mouth and the will. She was feeling like Kime would die to himself, but the thought of the difference in culture and telling him what she was feeling almost gagged her. How would she bring up the subject of sex to him? It is easier to do than to talk to him about it.

The ugly war waged; it was a horrific time of waiting before Nirma could talk with Kime again, and two weeks later, Nirma saw an opening to chat. Her bungalow was next to his. She saw Kime in passing.

"We need to get together again. I realize I didn't answer some of your questions, and I didn't want to be rude," she said.

"Okay, tomorrow at three, good for you?" replied Kime.

"Yes." She nodded.

The officers club was not crowded, and the corner spot was perfect. Kime pulled up the chair for her; Nirma took note of that. "You are probably wondering why I didn't answer your questions totally, aren't you?" she said.

He gazed into her eyes.

"I don't like the military, though I love America," she said.

"I could tell you're being in the military wasn't that simple," he said. "Your files don't even begin to explain who you are."

Maybe he's seeing in my heart, she thought. "I hate injustice!" she said.

"Is that why the thesis?"

"Yes, partly."

"Why make it so complex and symbolic?"

"Because I am complex, look again," she told hm.

"This die/kill stuff is symbolic, isn't it?" Kime asked once more.

Nirma saw Kime relax as she emptied her heart. Oh, she had been dying for this. *Oops.* She caught herself saying *dying,* and she thought of the symbolism. Just maybe she didn't have to kill anyone. He was dying to himself.

"So you came into the military to further work on your thesis or to take revenge on the military or did you come to the military to find me?" said Kime.

She giggled. "Ha! You wish."

She had feelings she couldn't express because of culture; she wanted him now but couldn't tell him. She decided to stay away from him for a while.

*****

Three weeks later, she was missing him. She saw Rom, her fellow Eskimo soldier, in the officer's tent. "Rom, I need your help with Kime. We are having a culture clash."

Rom was the chief of his village, and when off duty, people would flock to him. He was on the short side and looked like a monk.

"What do you mean?" he asked.

Nirma hung her head down.

Finally, Rom said, "Come on, talk, give it a shot."

"I am too ashamed," Nirma said. "You know in our culture women don't talk to men about sex, especially to a man of a different culture. This is affecting our relationship."

"Good, you are talking about it to me. That's one baby step. Don't let your culture mess it up with this guy, take another baby step," Rom asserted.

"He is otherwise perfect, Rom," she said.

"Culture needs to be out of the way of love," Rom said. "If he is as perfect as you say, he will be patient with you until you learn to communicate about sex or anything. I will have a talk with Kime and tell him I talked with you. Get past your pride and communicate, Nirma."

"*Pride*! Are you kidding me?" Nirma screamed.

Several days passed after Kime had seen Nirma and Rom talking several times. Rom approached Kime. Nirma overheard Rom say, "Kime, Kime, you have a minute?" Kime kept walking. At dinner that evening, Nirma sat at a different table all by herself. She wondered what was Kime thinking after seeing her talking to Rom. She saw Kime leaving the hall. Nirma caught on. Kime was jealous. She liked that. She let out a laugh.

Army business brought them together the next day. Nirma didn't have to muster up courage. She walked right up to Kime and said, "Rom has reconnected us."

"I agree," he said. "I understand the symbolism 'die or I will kill you,' Nirma. You don't have to kill me. I get it. I will die to myself and put you first. Patience is my middle name."

Nirma thought of her days of marching and a plaything, and relief was setting in like a pill. She flung her hands up in the air, winked at him, and walked away skipping. She heard, *At last ...* resounding in her ears. She bent down to pick up her pen and was raised up by Allstate hands wrapped around her waist tightly. She looked at him approvingly. She squealed! She locked the moment in her mind; she looked at him approvingly. She didn't have to kill him. Faith restored in men, she saw herself in his arms long after the Army was a distant memory.

BAFFLED, BRUISED IDIOT

Bobby walked into his Martha Stewart–decorated kitchen and wiped the forks, even the in-between of the forks. He was Mr. Mom to his three kids in their lakeside Vermont home. His wife, Catherine, would pick at anything when it came to him. The kitchen was a place to hide out. He was tired of this nitpicking. Some days he felt like just getting the hell outta there. Living like this was like a drum filling up one drop at a time—*drip, drip, drip*. Her nitpicking were gnats that kept hitting him from every direction. He felt bruised by the drips and nits. Nits were like gnats on a swampy beach. Catherine even told him he was an idiot. The respect he got from leading a team of twenty scientists was ancient as Noah and the ark. This Monday was one day before his unemployment check would run out. Talking to Catherine about almost anything, understanding her, and figuring out what would make her happy was like trying to get into a vault in the Pentagon. His goal to understand and please her was as huge as the Pacific Ocean.

The phone rang, and it was Wendy, a headhunter. Bobby spoke as Catherine was coming in the room.

"Who was that?" she asked.

"Some job lead," he said.

"I meant, *who* is it you were talking to, Bobby?"

"Wendy."

"Who is Wendy?" Catherine glared below her glasses.

Oh boy! Here she goes, he thought.

"A headhunter referring me for a job at Glaze Gym."

For months, Catherine had brought home the paycheck from her minimum-wage receptionist job. All she did there was look pretty and act nice; that was natural for her. The work balance in her home was like the Titanic starting to sink. It was six times Bobby had heard, "No, I am tired," from her. Her constant promise was making him look like a fool. Bobby told her last week she was Mrs. Ice Queen. He was more baffled at home than he was in his complex genetics research.

But Wendy's recommendation finally paid off. It was the first week on his new job. Bobby pulled up to the hill and saw the gym, and his eyes grew big. He paused and looked over the beautiful, nationally famous fall foliage in the green mountains of Vermont. It looked like some great painter took all their colors and splashed them against a giant canvas down below. He always had a love for art.

Training went well for three weeks. On the morning of the fourth week, Bobby was well into the session with his first client. It was Wendy, of all people. *What is she doing here?* he wondered.

Wendy was busting where Catherine was sagging after three kids. Her blue sports bra strained to keep her upper body from distracting men like Bobby. It appeared to others that she should be a trainer herself. He heard her groan in-between arm raises, without a pause. He watched Wendy noticing his muscular build. It wasn't the first time a woman had checked him out.

Wendy said in rapid succession, "Were you and your wife coming to the Halloween party here? What are you going to dress up as? Are you coming alone? I would love to see you there."

"Mmmm," said Bobby. The line of questioning and the moment felt like when he and Catherine were dating. Wendy's eyes stayed on his muscular arms.

"Where did your Latin accent come from?" she asked.

Why is she asking me these questions? He did not want to engage in the conversation. "Los Angeles," he said.

"Were you always interested in being a trainer?"

"No, I always wanted to be a scientist."

His mind flashed through several scenarios, and he looked away briefly. She closed her eyes to exhale. His body started to quiver as he tried to shake off his thoughts and feelings that were starting to strangle him. His heartbeat was getting faster. The thumping in his ears was louder than her exhaling. She was no ice queen. His thoughts about Catherine couldn't drum out the question whether she was paying attention to him. It hit him like a lightning bolt.

*****

Bobby was smart, but it plagued him as to how he would explain to Catherine about the work. She was bound to ask. Anything for her to gain some sense of security. The weekend was here. All was quiet in living room. The glass window gave a clear view of the lake with the full moon rising. Catherine was lounged across the couch in her pj's. Bobby noticed her body was relaxed, but he could see that pensive look on her face. He could tell that thoughts were firing in her head.

"Bobby, come here!" she blurted as she turned off the TV.

He sized up the scene and hurried over to her.

Catherine spoke without glancing at him. "How is the job going? I am so tired at nights, I am thinking all these things. I don't want to work this low-paying job anymore. I am thinking also, maybe I shouldn't have married you."

Her comments hit Bobby dead-on like a missile. He stared at the ceiling and then hung his head. It was as if his answer meant the difference between scot-free and the death chamber. His deep-furrowed brow revealed his thoughts.

Catherine broke the almost eerie silence. "And I am thinking that I am not being such a good mom also."

Bobby was still trying to process her earlier comments. Still, he was glad she was talking. Usually he would just sit, run his mouth, and get defensive. Her critical comment would lash out like a whip.

"Well, work is …," and he paused as Wendy popped into his head.

"Work is what?" demanded Catherine. "Come on, spit it out. I can read you like a book. I am a woman and one who has known you for eighteen years!"

Bobby felt the vice grip slowly turning. He noticed that Catherine sat up straight and looked away in silence.

"Honey, I love you." He reached for her hands. The awkwardness on the sofa was like an impregnated silence. "Work just continues to go well," he said.

Dates were few and far between. Catherine's moods continued to be like the rapids on the Colorado River. Bobby thought a movie would be a good idea.

"Hon, how about going to the theatre on Saturday night?"

"Okay, there is one I saw advertised. *Don't Touch My Nightmare*—that sounds interesting," she said.

"Sounds intriguing," he replied as he wondered how someone could touch a nightmare. "What about this woman in the movie and her nightmare. Seems she was talking about more than just a nightmare?"

"Ya, sure," Catherine muttered under her breath. "I don't know, it feels weird. Forget it, your questions are exhausting me."

She stormed out of the room.

*****

At work the next day, the sunlight pierced the room, and Bobby noticed Wendy checking her stats. She whistled as she walked his way.

"Hey, Bobby, can I talk to you after our session?"

"Sure," he said. Then later Wendy came up to him.

"Bobby, can you come be my personal trainer at my house gym, two hours a day, and I will give you a $20,000 retainer?"

Bobby gave it some thought. Two women bossing him around, "Bobby come here," "Bobby do this," "Bobby do that." But twenty thousand dollars would make Catherine feel better.

"Yes," he said at last.

Soon afterward, he called Catherine.

"Hey, hon, I got a second job being a trainer at my client Wendy's home. I get twenty thousand dollars up front."

"Great," said Catherine.

"Okay, you can start next Wednesday," said Wendy when Bobby got off the phone with a yes.

On the way home, a marriage conference announcement was blaring on the radio. *Maybe a nice drive and a weekend away would do us great,* Bobby thought.

Later that night, he said, "Hey, hon, how about going to this marriage conference in Maine?"

No answer.

"Honey, did you hear me?"

"I am not deaf!" she crossed her arms. "I don't like those things," she yelled.

"Give it a try, hon," said Bobby.

"Well, all right already." Catherine said between her teeth.

*****

Bobby packed the car long before he went to work Friday morning. It was early Saturday as he drove. He saw Catherine's gaze was focused on the dashboard as she snuggled down in to the bench seat. Bobby wished she would cozy up to him. He felt that her nodding off was a way to avoid intimacy and conversation. Her shifting made her dress hike up to show her long nimble leg. Bobby took a deep breath as he glanced at his wife. *Mmmm!*

She stared as if Bobby wasn't even there.

"Isn't this exciting, hon? Just the two of us, like starting over again," said Bobby as he touched her. "That is what this conference is geared to do."

Catherine didn't even move.

He saw her eyes widened as the car pulled into Amor Conference Center. The driveway was lined with red valentine balloons and red roses. The check-in lounge had videos of couples holding hands and love songs were playing. Everything was in gear if only Catherine would get onboard.

Bobby escorted her up the elevator. The windows in the rooms were all facing the foliage. A fireplace warmed the living room. The bedroom had a large Jacuzzi lined with oils and scents from exotic countries. As Bobby unpacked the suitcase, he caught Catherine peeking into the bathroom. His mind wandered. Bobby could tell her hesitation as he headed into the amphitheater.

A middle-aged woman got up to the lectern. "My name is Pam. I am a professor of anthropology from Barbados, and I am the author of *Don't Touch My Nightmare*. Our format this weekend is lecture-feedback-practice. Practice starts tonight, and session ends on Sunday." The room filled with nervous laughter. Amidst the laughter, Bobby noticed Catherine rolling her eyes. Pam continued, "I am here to tell you marriage takes hard work."

Bobby turned to Catherine, and their eyes mated.

During the break, Bobby had a quizzical look on his face. "Hey, hon, I still don't get the nightmare thing."

"Well, this weekend will not be a loss if you learned that. You will see."

*****

After the first session, Bobby sat with Catherine in the lounge.

"Bobby, this is actually refreshing. I am glad you made me come," said Catherine.

Bobby, with a big grin on his face, felt ready to engage. Stepping into the elevator that evening after the feedback session, he experienced mounting joy as he felt Catherine's hands slipping into his.

"For years, we had been roommates. You didn't know me," said Catherine. "When my heart is closed, other parts of me is closed off too. If I like you standing up, I will like you lying down. Intimacy with a stranger frightens me. That is my nightmare."

Bobby squeezed her hands, and his face lit up.

"I want to really know you," he said.

"I might let you touch my nightmare later during practice," she told him.

"Got it, Cath."

Practice went well.

Then it was late afternoon, and they were on their way home. Bobby's thoughts were overflowing, and the car was silent. Out of nowhere, Catherine's comment broke the silence.

"I like the money, especially the retainer already cashed, but watch out for that Wendy woman and her nightmare."

"You got it," he said.

*****

Several days of the part-time job at Wendy's house passed. Bobby wrapped up the session with laps in the pool. He watched Wendy slip out and put a towel around her stringed bikini. While seeing himself out, he stopped at the door.

"Hey, Wendy, do you live in this beautiful mansion by yourself? All I see is you and the dogs."

"Want to see the house?" she said with raised eyebrows.

What the heck, he thought, and he followed her like a puppy.

The ten-room house was like a museum. The living room had tall ceilings with spiral staircase, Degas paintings on the walls, and thick Persian rugs you were afraid to walk on. As Bobby's eyes were admiring the paintings in the rooms, Wendy's eyes were focused on him. The clock was ticking and so was Bobby's taste for art. A red flag went off in his head, but he deleted it. Eight beautiful rooms went by.

Petals on the floor? That's strange, he thought. It was like going down a slippery slope. This room was facing the lake. Curiosity trumped his weariness. The room was exquisitely decorated with an antique bed that had mirrors over it, inviting you to lie down. The sunlight reflecting from the lake was a work of art itself. Bobby thought briefly of Catherine and Amor and quickly dismissed it. Just then, he remembered that Wendy did not answer the question he asked at the front door, and here he was. Bobby reflected on the conference. He realized he should have paid attention to the heart when it came to women.

Suddenly, the door locked behind him, and Wendy stood there. The room sat heavy with tension as the silence lingered. His mind didn't even have a chance to disengage out of his blur! Wendy dropped all her clothes, down to her bikini.

"I see you like art," she said. "This is the ultimate art!"

He stood transfixed, not knowing what to do with his eyes; his body shivered. His emotions and thoughts chased each other around the globe. He saw something he was not expecting as her eyes were trying to seduce him by what he saw. He saw her bend down, quickly take the towel, and wrap it around her body.

"I think this session is over!" said Wendy as she put on her sweat suit and ushered him quickly to the door. "I hope this doesn't make you quit on the retainer. See you tomorrow."

Bobby said goodbye and didn't even look back.

The drive to home was like a scene out of a love mystery movie. His knuckles were white as he drove and he thought about sitting down with Catherine. Her conversation the night before was like a broken record in his head.

*****

That night Bobby overheard Catherine on the phone say, "I would love to see you, Wendy. Next Thursday at 4:00 p.m. is good." His blood pressure rose as he pondered what he heard. He lay in bed that night staring at the ceiling wanting to ask her which Wendy, but dared not.

Next day, Bobby pulled up to Wendy's gate, pressed the code, and sat there. His mind was no friend to him. She was waiting in her gym when he got there. His eyes were on a clothed Wendy, but his mind was flashing images of the ultimate art. It was like he was standing in quicksand.

"Are you okay, Bobby?" Wendy asked.

What game is she playing? he thought. "What was that in the bedroom yesterday?" he asked.

"You came on to me, Bobby, getting into my heart," she told him.

"Came on to you! *What*! I was just shooting the breeze asking about your house."

"Well, your arrow went straight into my heart." She let that sink in. "I told you yesterday it was art, Bobby. Maybe it was also a message that I want to be open, be naked, and share what was in my heart."

Right! thought Bobby.

"Why are women so complex?"

"Ask your wife."

"I am just trying to learn how to understand her, and now here we are. This might not be a good time to have that conversation."

Wendy pulled back from the fifteen-minute chat at the door, sat down, and began to sob.

Uh-oh! Bobby thought, *What now?*

"When Tom left me last year, I was shattered, empty, and lost," she said. "I tried art, and I am trying lifestyle change with you and the gym. I am trying to take care of my body, mind, and spirit."

Fifteen minutes later, Bobby had no words. The best he did was what she needed and what he mustered up, listening and affirming her.

Wendy continued, "I knew there was something special about you and that I could trust you. Tell your wife that."

Bobby thought, *You got to be kidding me!* Breaking this news to Catherine would be as hard as the president sharing the secrets of his daily security briefing.

"Thanks for coming today," Wendy said. "This was my workout, the best so far."

On the way to Glaze, Bobby pulled the car over and just sat there.

Later that night in the bathroom, he could overhear Catherine on the phone say, "I just want to thank you for helping me, Wendy."

What in the world was she talking about? He took up the razor to shave, stumbled, and dropped it.

*****

It was 9:30 p.m. Bobby had his pjs on. He cautiously crept into the alcove leading into the living room while wiping his brow, his bare feet brushing the Persian rug. At the other end of the room was Catherine sitting on the love seat. The sight of her still not dressed for bed caused his anxiety to soar. The walls lined with bookshelves were his shield. He wondered why she was not in her pjs. His hands shaking, his mind racing, he reached for the manual from the marriage conference. *Boy, I could use Pam right now,* he thought. He stood there glancing over at Catherine. He felt like he was standing before a senate hearing only this time she was the senator in chief who was sitting there devoted to doing her nails. The heavy silence was broken, and suddenly the doorbell rang.

"Bobby please get the door," said Catherine. She didn't even look up.

I am in my pj's and you are dressed, he said to himself. He dared not say it out loud. "Just a minute," said Bobby as he dragged some clothes on.

He pulled at the oak door, and there was Wendy. His eyes flew open. He stood there gasping out his mouth and barely able to speak.

"Honey, it's Wendy."

"I know," said Catherine as she smirked.

I know! What kind of attitude was that? The thought of what would happen next was like being led to a firing squad.

"Hi, Bobby," said Wendy as she walked on past him and embraced Catherine.

He stood there with his mouth open, trying to recover.

"Aren't you coming over, Bobby?" asked Catherine.

He moved like a dog on a leash.

"Sit between us," she said as she pointed with a half-smile.

There was an awkward silence before the bomb dropped.

Catherine said, "I have known Wendy for twenty years. I got her to hook you up with both the job at Glaze and at her house. She tested you for me to see if you could learn to understand me. You passed the test and were found faithful." Bobby felt his temperature rising as he jerked his hands away from Catherine for a brief moment. She quickly reached to take back his hands.

"I love you, honey." She reached over and kissed him. He could see Wendy covering her eyes, and he soared in the embrace of his wife.

He didn't want to even remotely act baffled knowing his bruising days were over. His perception as an idiot was erased. Later that night, the phone rang, disturbing them. Bobby checked voice mail. It was his old boss offering him his job back.

Trapped in Roundabout Love

"The Misty Blue" love song by Dorothy Moore blared, and Sabatha cringed. She thought, *What if Mom saw me here?* She turned the corner and sat in the dark alley; the bulbs were out in some of the rooms of the houses around, but enough light showed through the cracked pane. She heard the cussing as the drug pushers passed by. It reminded her of the tumultuous days at home. "Self," she said, "damn, I am in trouble! My mom would kill me if she knew I was here, but it is no party at home either." She thought of Mom's knitted eyebrows; military tone; and agonizing, wandering look. A car backfired, but she heard a gunshot. She ducked. She immediately snapped back into the reality of the moment, and she got up and started to head home. The barraging thoughts flooded her mind. The fear oppressed her every step like a heavy weight on the entire journey.

As she opened the door, the blast of, "Sabatha, where have you been?" hit her point-blank. The agendas of Sabatha and her Mom collided like a bad train wreck. The urge for the alley grew insatiably and became a strong beast in her. Inside, her starving soul screamed, "I need to find love!" Exasperated, Mom blurted, "Where were you? Come here, you smell of wine, let me smell you." Sabatha just kept looking at her. The hate for this woman and the desire to please her waged a battle within her.

The next morning, a kind of artificial peace settled on Sabatha, but its instability was evident in her heart. Sabatha pulled up a chair to the dining room table to prepare for homeschooling. Completely dismissing the previous night's events, Mom got straight to business into homeschooling that morning.

An apprehensive Sabatha sat down as Mom opened up the health science book for the first lesson on hormones. Feeling trapped in the moment, Sabatha reluctantly listened as Mom began to speak of hormone release into the brain of a teenager relating to sexuality. Sabatha clearly caught Mom's tone change as she continued to teach on the role parents play in helping to shape and harness the surge of sexuality felt by the growing adolescent. Sabatha heard nothing of Mom's lecture after that moment. She wasn't even aware when the lecture ended and Mom left the table to start breakfast in the kitchen.

Mom had just cracked the egg when she heard Sabatha cry out with endearment, "Mommy!" from the other room. Rushing into the classroom, Mom's heart pounded, and her mind raced to connect with this small glimpse of her little girl—a little girl who had long since hidden behind a wall when Mom's control began so many years ago.

Staring at the table, Sabatha quietly volunteered, "You have been so good to me, in protecting me. I understand why you have been so strict." After a long pause, she looked up at her mom's face, and no longer did she see the knitted eyebrows. The softness that exuded cracked open the door into Sabatha's heart.

Stories of Sabatha's escapades began gushing out of her like a broken dam; the unloading to Mom was like a therapy session. With tears in her eyes, Sabatha glimpsed Mom out of the corner of her eye slowly and gently making her way to her daughter.

Wiping her eyes vigorously, Sabatha tried not to show she was crying. The tear-stained lesson of the day in front of her released evidence of her tears anyway. As Mom gently reached over and gave her little girl a hug, Sabatha's anxiety began to dissolve in her mother's arms, a feeling that had eluded her for quite some time. Sabatha heard in a quiet whisper, "Sabatha, you have touched my heart today in so many ways. Today I find new hope in me and in us."

In the still dark of her room, Sabatha lay on her bed staring at the ceiling, her temperature rising with each thought of the man back at the alley. The smell of perfume was in the air, and the soft bellowing of "Misty Blue" was playing again in her head. Slipping away into the eerie darkness, Sabatha paid no thought to her mom as she obeyed her lust and headed toward "Misty Blue."

Her head spinning from the day's emotional episode, Sabatha's confidence in her mom's genuineness of emotions began to fade, and the doubt crept in once again. As the noise of the alley grew stronger, all thoughts and hope that Mom was even able to change were squelched.

Arriving at the alley, all thoughts of mom disappeared as Sabatha's view hones in on one man, Mitch, smoking in the doorway. If home life was a cage, in Sabatha's mind, Mitch had the key to set her free, if only for a short while. All it took was Mitch's crooked smile for Sabatha to find herself transported, transfixed, and levitated in his car. "Where are you taking me?" Her question hung in the air as she showed no resistance to his driving down the lonely road to his rented duplex, only miles away from Sabatha's house.

Men like Mitch were the ones making Mom uneasy. Mitch had long known the tension at home and moved to take advantage of that, making passes at a vulnerable Sabatha. These passes were the only resemblance of love Sabatha knew. As the car pulled into the driveway, the rise of anxiety in Sabatha made her body grow tense. Sensing the tension, Mitch responded, and Sabatha felt the warmth of his arms around her as he whispered, "Relax, my wife is away at a conference." Mitch continued to titillate her ears with his smooth talk, all the while turning the key to unlock the cage. Where confusion once ruled, now her mind took on one focus—her desire for the strong man embracing and caressing her.

Sabatha showed no objection as he led her by the hand into the house. If this was just an illusion of love, Sabatha would take that over nothing and didn't want it to end. The touching and caressing that ensued awakened Sabatha. Her body engaged in all new experiences. Slowly, the confusion seeped in, *Is this what I am missing? Is this what real love feels like?* Confusion completely vanished as her body convulsed as the cage was now wide open, and for a moment, Sabatha was free as the orgasm exploded and dominated her whole being.

Moments later, Sabatha, her body sapped of all energy, came off the high and again found herself back in the cage full of guilt and fear. Feeling alone with her consuming thoughts, Sabatha lay in the dark next to Mitch. She quickly snapped back into the present when the sound of a door opened downstairs. As footsteps ascended the stairs, Sabatha scrambling to get her clothes on, heard Mitch across the room, "Damn, my wife's back early!"

The bedroom door opened, and the mistress's petrified eyes met the shocked and vengeful glare of the wife. Mitch's lame and fumbled explanations became merely background noise for the inevitable battle that was brewing between the two women. Sabatha, feeling the sting of her stare, heard the name "Bitch!" hurled at her like a machete. The wife, grabbing a pair of scissors off the dresser, lunged at her; and Sabatha bolted. She got only as far as the front door before Mitch's wife caught up to her, scissors still firmly in her grip. She ripped what clothes she could off Sabatha's fighting body and furiously shredded them to pieces. Sabatha barely escaped in time to hear her cry out, "Come back, and I'll kill you!"

Heart ponding and out of breath, terror washed over Sabatha crouched behind an alley dumpster, the only refuge she could find in the thick, lonely darkness. Finally, overcome with fear, she called the only comfort she knew—her mom. The familiar voice answered, and Sabatha strained to speak, "Mom, help. I was with a friend and—"

Her worried mom quickly insisted, "And what?"

"Someone wants to kill me. Help, come get me!" Sabatha pleaded.

"Who wants to kill you, Sabatha?"

A long pause followed, and Sabatha finally volunteered, "His wife."

With those two words, the anxious tone in Mom's voice quickly turned to one of rage. "You whore! That's it, Sabatha! It's clear you just don't care. How could you do this to me? You're out of here!" The silence on the other end of the line that followed Mom's hang up brought a desperation and sorrow to Sabatha's soul so oppressive that she simply dropped to her knees and sobbed.

Gaining composure, the brisk wind that chilled her scantily clad body awakened her that she'd better find shelter soon. Sabatha had reached the end of her rope and stood at the doorway of a long-ago acquaintance, one whom she had not spoken to for over a decade. In her desperation, she prayed this would work. When the door finally opened and she saw the look of shock slowly turn to a smile of recognition, she knew she had found a refuge, at least for a little while.

Two weeks went by, and Sabatha had now worn out her welcome. With no money, no hope, and no other options, she ended up back at mom's doorstep like a starving, humble puppy looking for a scrap anyone had to give.

As the door opened, Sabatha braced herself for the anticipated raging outburst. Instead, to her surprise, she was met with a face much calmer in disposition standing in front of her. Mom stared at Sabatha, as if trying to find answers to so many long-standing questions that haunted her.

Her mom, desperately trying to hide the tear welling up in her eye, moved to embrace her daughter, her little girl, the one she so desperately wanted to control and protect all at the same time.

In the silence of the embrace, Mom became, once again, a stop on the that familiar roundabout that Sabatha always felt herself on, always moving, always seeking, getting bits and pieces of love from Mom and men but never really going anywhere. Here she was again back in her trap. *Oh well*, Sabatha thought, *Mom's scraps are better than nothing*, and she embraced her mother back.

Love between Two Candlesticks

From the blackjack table, Helva's call of nature spoke, and a fast-paced strut ensued to the ladies' room. Inside, the fragrance of the lilies filled her nostrils. The plush, inviting couch made the room seem more like a suite than a bathroom. Her surroundings, however, could not subdue what she was feeling and thinking.

Shifting flickers of thoughts invaded her head. Helva stood paralyzed before the opulent mirror, her eyes fixed on the reflection. The face she saw was not her own. The one looking back at her was cold and empty. She couldn't see how her tumultuous life with Fred, her husband, could possibly change. Years of not being allowed to share her feelings with Fred and him not listening to her had caused their intimacy to fade and love to stop flowing. Brow furrowed, the weight of all those wasted years of emptiness and regrets ate her like cancer.

Finally, Helva stormed out the door, knocking over two candlesticks on the way back to Fred at the blackjack table. Her husband, Fred, was an information technology executive and was a very quiet guy. Her anger exploded as she sat down and looked at Fred and spoke through her teeth. "I have been such a *fool.*"

"Mmmm … what's the matter?" asked Fred lamely.

"Don't touch me!" she said as Fred reached out, fumbling to comfort her. She glared at the dealer as he dealt her cards. She screamed, "I was a fool to have chased you."

No answer from Fred, just blank looks.

"Well, say something for yourself," she said seethingly, raising her voice. "All these years you led me on, I finally saw it in the mirror."

"What mirror?" Fred whispered as the dealer dealt the cards.

"You don't know the half of it, a lot more where that came from." Helva threw her cards across the table, causing consternation to the couple sitting there. She could feel her body stiffen, her eyes shooting insults, looking defiant; and with a hiss, she strutted across the floor and out the door at midnight, wanting to be alone. Helva had come to the island with her husband, Fred, to jump-start their love flow. American Virgin Island, known as America's paradise had seemed the perfect place. She set out for a long walk hoping to get solace and guidance to work out their problems and have their love flow again.

As she walked on the beach, the golden full moon gliding above was the only gauge of time. The waves at midnight were pounding the shore, rushing in and out like her turbulent thoughts. The sound of the thundering of the waves echoed in her, steadily rising her rage. The imprint of her feet in the sand could have captured her DNA if it weren't that the waves washed away each of her agonized steps. With every stride, she flung her hands from side to side like a soldier under orders.

As she recalled the moment in front of the mirror, the same nauseating pang in her stomach snatched her and made her want to vomit. She picked up a broken watch washed ashore by the waves and thought painfully of her own brokenness. The moon changed positions as she followed the outline of the beach; her mind changing with each curve. The breezy condition tamed the tropical ninety-degree heat, but not the anger inside her, which was like a volcano. The journey continued until exhaustion trumped anger. Her shaky legs collapsed on the beach, and she soon, fell asleep.

Helva woke up wondering, *Where am I?* She saw the figure of a man approaching her in the door. She jumped. "Who the hell are you?" she asked.

"My name is Maurice. I found you on the beach," he said.

She studied him out of the corner of her eye. She tried helplessly to remain clam, feeling knotted up inside. She wondered how and when she got there and what had she missed.

"What happened to you?" he said.

"Long story! You don't want to know," she replied, fidgeting her fingers and staring at the floor.

"What brought you to the island?" he asked.

Helva didn't respond, hoping he would stop the interrogation. She saw a warm smile come across his face, and he changed direction of the conversation. "Can I get you something to eat and a change of clothes?"

She muttered a stiff, "Thank you."

He gently handed her a dry shirt to change into and went in the kitchen.

As she unbuttoned her wet clothes, Helva thought, *Maybe he is safe.* She wanted to believe it. The smell of the curry coming from the kitchen reminded her of home. Her tension starting to ease.

"Do you live alone?" Helva called out.

"Yes, with my dog!" he replied.

"So do you have a girlfriend?" she asked courageously.

"I don't date," Maurice said soberly.

Intrigued, Helva said, "Really!"

"I am a monk," he told her.

Now Helva felt really safe. Her pulsed quickened, and a steady heat rose from inside her as feelings were aroused—feelings that she had not felt in years. She reached forward to gently touch him. He pulled back.

"I am here as your caretaker, but I can do no more than that."

Helva had no words. She simply shook her head. She watched him go out the room and heard him yell out the window, "Ella! Come here."

Who is Ella? Helva thought. She saw her own reflection in the mirror in the hallway. She was startled, and she said to herself, *Who are you anyway?*

Ella reached out to Helva and gave her a big hug. It turned out she was the island's mystic, a parapsychologist sort who reminded you of a flower child of the Woodstock era.

Helva's heart raced. With a groan in her soul, she started weeping. The flood of tears started like scorching lava busting forth and flowing down the mountain. She wept uncontrollably as she clung to

Ella. Helva felt Ella's soft breath and the rise and fall of her chest as she held her close till her pain started to subside.

Ella said, "I can feel your pain."

Helva thought, *This is someone I can trust.* Her heart jolted like a bolt of lightning, and she stood there speechless.

"We must go to Mongo," Ella said. Helva looked up at her with shifted eyes. Ella patted her on the arm and said, "Trust me!"

Helva instinctively knew she could trust her. Mongo was the island's priest and guru, who was known for peering into people's soul. His nightly meetings were well attended by island folks. Everyone knew him.

Maurice overheard them and said, "Let me take you there by boat."

The trip to Mongo's took thirty minutes. As they got closer to Mongo's place, the music there became clearer and clearer. It was melodious and enchanting. The drum beat in the distant made you want to get there faster. Helva felt a blissful rush in her soul. She said to herself, *What the heck, I might as well join them.*

As the boat pulled up to the dock, the heavy beat of the music resonated inside Helva's chest. She stepped onto the shore and saw a large figure of a man approaching her, his long dreadlocks swinging with each step. He had a twinge of graying in the black locks. The beads around his neck was a representation of every color in the rainbow. His eyes were hazel and inviting. Helva heard someone say, "Mongo is highly revered." Her eyes met his deep soulful approaching stare, and although she had never met the man, something comfortable and familiar pierced her soul.

"I've been expecting you," he said, his voice as melodious as the music. Helva felt the warmth of his hand as he gently touched her on the head and mumbled something unintelligible into her ear. A quiet calm rushed over here. *Is he for real?* she thought.

"What are you feeling?" Mongo prompted.

No words came. It was as if the numbness was getting broken up in her by his simple melodic words.

"Get in touch," Mongo continued, holding his palm to her heart.

The music grew louder in her ears and inside her, resounding and vibrating, her racing heartbeat keeping time with the ever-increasing beat of the island drums. Louder, harder until heat permeated her body as if the light had broken free and was now infiltrating every cell in her body.

"Are you feeling the flow?" Mongo whispered. "The flow of love?"

"Awesome, yes!" Helva wanted to cry, but no sound came. She was overwhelmed by the healing light being unleashed inside her. Speechless, she stood, and her mind raced as her heart (emotional heart) leapt, her brain sending signals. Her spirit exploded in her heart, and her emotions overtook her; all a part of her activated self. Eyes transfixed on Mongo, she could not help but think, *It's like he's seeing right into my heart!* It was a very frightening yet comforting experience. Confusion caused her both elation and fear.

She felt an uncomfortable pressure in her chest as her heart seemed to grow bigger. The haunting voids left by bitterness were saturated with hope-filled light. Helva felt like her chest would burst, and tears flowed as the hardness melted—the light softening everything it touched. Anger gone, bitterness gone, and in their place stood growing hope. A deep security softened, and feeling cherished washed over her like a child protected by daddy's strong arms.

As the tears dropped, so did her guard and words gushed out her mouth to Mongo like torrential rain, "I am free, I am free!" Everything was leaving her now out her heart, out her mouth until no remnant of hidden darkness remained.

Mongo said, "All secrets are coming to light, and all that remains is light. He stood intently listening and then responded quietly, "This is the greatest part of healing, leading to love flow. It's all about relationship. Now, Helva, where does it need to go?"

Deep inside, Helva heard, *Cincinnati!*

"The remainder of love will flow now," Mongo whispered.

Helva's body filled with excitement like being intoxicated, her heart beating wildly. Mind transcending, she fell to the ground, only this time it was different.

Suddenly, like an eclipse, all was gone. Helva sat up in the hammock at the cottage, her eyes frantically scanning the room. "Where's Mongo? Where's Ella?" she said out loud. Sweating profusely, she faintly heard Maurice ask, "Who's Mongo?"

"Take me to the hotel now!" she demanded. She knew what she had to do.

Rushing into the lobby, Helva pleaded with the front desk about her husband's whereabouts. Despite Helva's tangled and sweat-drenched hair and bruised face, the clerk recognized her from the fliers around town. Then he remembered Fred leaving her cell phone at the front desk on the desperate chance that she returned. He quickly ran to retrieve it and gave it to Helva. With trembling fingers, Helva fumbled to read the text message saying, "Emergency at home WILL RETURN to find you—CALL ME PLEASE IF YOU GET THIS." Hastily, she jumped back into the car. "To the airport!" she screamed to a waiting Maurice.

Thoughts of Fred flooded her mind, and glancing thought the rearview mirror, she saw a different woman. Outside her window, the vast ocean was rhythmically lapping on the shore. *God, keep this ocean here in my heart. Help the current to flow in me. God, you know I love him,* she thought.

At the airport, Maurice asked, "What happened to you back there?"

"I don't know what happened, but I can see clearly now. The darkness has lifted," and with a quick hug and a few tears, she was on her way back home to Cincinnati.

Fred's car was not in the driveway when the taxi pulled up to her house. Inside the dark house, the morning's coffee sat cold on the kitchen counter where Fred had left it. Not knowing when he would return, Helva quickly put her plan to action with the groceries she picked up. When Fred wouldn't leave her mind and she could stand it no longer, *I'm going to call him!* she thought. Her heart raced as she dialed her cell phone and the other end rang.

Helva heard a frantic, "Hello? Helva, is that you?"

"Yes!" she cried, tears streaming down her face. "I'm home!

"What? Oh, thank God! How? Why?" Fred couldn't finish his thoughts, and finally, he cried, "Honey, I'll be home in an hour! I fixed the problem here."

Helva stood before the mirror. Her favorite CD was playing in the background, and the lyrics sunk into her like a sponge: "I can see clearly now the rain is gone ..." back-to-back with "At last my love has come along." Hope filled her like the savory aroma of Fred's favorite surf-and-turf dish filled the house. Everything had been well-thought-out and planned right down to the gold utensils and the red tablecloth covered in hearts and angel figures. Two candlesticks with dancing flames provided the light on the dinner table—one on her end and one on Fred's. Her dress, so hastily thrown on, had settled delicately on her frame, and her hair fell softly around her shoulders, loose curls flowed just the way Fred liked it. She sat there pondering the moment.

Fred came running up the front walkway. The door flew open to the house, as did the door to Helva's heart. Peering through the candlesticks, she saw Fred in a new way. His arms around her, Helva knew she was where she belonged. Heart-to-heart conversation went on for three hours. As the last of the candle flame succumbed to its end over dinner, Helva yawned and headed up the stairway, and with a playful grin across her face, she spoke softly, "Coming up?" Love began to flow again, started in paradise and between the candle sticks.

About the Author

Oren L. Harris is a relationship counselor who has created the ELLER (Experiencing Long-Lasting and Enjoyable Relationships) model. His true passion is to see people find love perfectly and have love flowing forever. He believes that far too many relationships are long-lasting and not enjoyable or not enjoyable as when one first found love. So as a counselor, he is also a behaviorist, and researcher, problem-solver, a conflict resolution expert, a life coach, and an advisor.

Born in Jamaica, West Indies, Oren has lived in the northeastern United States for fifty-one years. During his twenty-five-year career, he has counseled couples and saved their marriages, as well as prevented people from staying in unhealthy relationships. He is a graduate of Stevens Institute of Technology and Carin University. Oren received a bachelor's in theology and leadership and a master's degree in management with thesis. In addition to operating his own counseling practice, Oren enjoys speaking engagements.

This is his first book. Oren has copyrighted the ELLER model—registered and trade marked ELLER as a brand. A relationship/counseling model designed to provide people with practical tools and resources to build strong relationships in order to avoid heartbreaks, affairs, and divorce.

CPSIA information can be obtained
at www.ICGtesting.com
Printed in the USA
LVHW011312020920
664818LV00005B/741